POWER NUGGETS

101 Reflections
For
Empowered Living

Mark Bowser

Fairway Press, Lima, Ohio

POWER NUGGETS

FIRST EDITION
Copyright © 1999 by
Mark Bowser

Library of Congress Catalog Card Number: 98-93822

ISBN 0-7880-1424-2
PRINTED IN U.S.A.

I lovingly dedicate this book to my Lord and Savior Jesus Christ who makes all things possible and to Sarah, the wonderful gift He has blessed me with.

Table Of Contents

Introduction

SECTION ONE: A New Beginning

POWER NUGGET #1: In the beginning of time, God created the earth and along with it man and woman, and He bestowed greatness with each one, a greatness unique to each individual which, if developed, will shape the world to righteousness.

POWER NUGGET #2: Make sure what goes into your mind is positive because what comes out is always what went in.

POWER NUGGET #3: We are all beautiful in the eyes of God.

POWER NUGGET #4: Man must learn to crawl before he can walk and one must walk before he can run.

POWER NUGGET #5: Self-dignity and self-esteem are the greatest needs of every individual. Respect and love for oneself is vital for survival and a happy fulfilling life.

POWER NUGGET #6: Self-love is the kind of love that motivates a person to greatness.

POWER NUGGET #7: When it is all said and done, at the heart of the champion is LOVE!

POWER NUGGET #8: A man's actions choose his future.

POWER NUGGET #9: I have faith in Jesus Christ; therefore I am.

POWER NUGGET #10: A winner is not a perfect human being. There are no perfect human beings. A winner is an imperfect human being striving to be better.

POWER NUGGET #11: Patience is a weapon which can reveal miracles.

POWER NUGGET #12: PEACE — a calm emotion with tremendous strength.

POWER NUGGET #13: Jesus said to me, "Mark, no matter how many times the crucifixion is replayed, there is always one conclusion — THE RESURRECTION!"

POWER NUGGET #14: Everyone has a little child within him that needs to come out and play from time to time.

POWER NUGGET #15: Happiness is always created from the inside, not from the outside.

POWER NUGGET #16: Be happy where you are, but work toward the future.

POWER NUGGET #17: An idea is the greatest investment.

POWER NUGGET #18: Motivation without direction is dangerous. Motivation with positive direction is success!

POWER NUGGET #19: Hope is a little thing that carries big dividends in the journey of life.

POWER NUGGET #20: Integrity and character go hand and hand.

POWER NUGGET #21: Great strength comes from within, not from without.

POWER NUGGET #22: To me success is continually learning and growing and doing my very best always for Jesus Christ.

POWER NUGGET #23: There is no coincidence with God.

POWER NUGGET #24: Every day is your day ... and you've got what it takes!

POWER NUGGET #25: Leave it to God; He never fails.

POWER NUGGET #26: True beauty is a reflection of who you are, not from what you do (as in job or career) or what you look like.

POWER NUGGET #27: Curiosity is the uncovering mechanism to new discoveries.

POWER NUGGET #28: The man is not the ship; the ship is the *man*.

POWER NUGGET #29: The ship does not make the man; the *man* makes the ship.

POWER NUGGET #30: Commitment is a decision not a happenstance.

POWER NUGGET #31: Every sunrise is filled with the possibilities of a new day.

POWER NUGGET #32: You can have tremendous health and energy ALL your life!

POWER NUGGET #33: Each day is a new opportunity to succeed.

POWER NUGGET #34: The roadmap is the dream; the road is the goal; and putting it into action is the vehicle that makes it go.

POWER NUGGET #35: It is not as important WHERE you are going as it is WHY you are going there. The why has got to lead the where.

POWER NUGGET #36: To live an empowered life character is a requirement, not a choice.

SECTION TWO: The Road That Leads To Success

POWER NUGGET #37: Help someone love him/herself and you have made a friend for life.

POWER NUGGET #38: FAITH — The great motivation!

POWER NUGGET #39: Boldness of faith conquers all defeat.

POWER NUGGET #40: See the opportunities! Seize the opportunities!

POWER NUGGET #41: Focused concentration creates breakthroughs in your life.

POWER NUGGET #42: Believe and succeed!

POWER NUGGET #43: Believe in yourself and people will begin to believe in you too.

POWER NUGGET #44: If you can't see the light at the end of the tunnel then light a match and create your own light with God's help.

POWER NUGGET #45: When you help others shoot for the moon you will then find yourself among the stars.

POWER NUGGET #46: Be a dreamer and an achiever.

POWER NUGGET #47: When things seem at their worst then REJOICE because there is only one direction to go — UP!

POWER NUGGET #48: The most powerful thing in the universe: A positive idea that is acted upon.

POWER NUGGET #49: JESUS CHRIST — The Great Dreamer!

POWER NUGGET #50: JESUS CHRIST — The Great Motivator!

POWER NUGGET #51: MAKE IT A GREAT DAY...WITH GOD!

POWER NUGGET #52: Sometimes the best thing to do is the hardest thing to do — "Wait on the Lord."

POWER NUGGET #53: When you ask God a question He will sometimes ask you questions which will lead to the answer you are pursuing.

POWER NUGGET #54: Obeying the Golden Rule is the sign of a positive high self-esteem: "Do unto others as you would like them to do unto you." (The Bible)

POWER NUGGET #55: Success is never created through doubt; success is always created through belief.

POWER NUGGET #56: It is better to err on the side of trust then to err on the side of judgmentalness.

POWER NUGGET #57: There is no success without Jesus Christ.

POWER NUGGET #58: You can't count your chickens before they hatch but you can at least keep the eggs warm.

POWER NUGGET #59: There is no success without risk.

POWER NUGGET #60: The strength of human beings lies in their integrity.

POWER NUGGET #61: Insecurity is an emotion which can only be conquered through faith.

POWER NUGGET #62: When excitement is created, creativity will always follow.

POWER NUGGET #63: To be successful, one must find the balance between patience and assertiveness.

POWER NUGGET #64: You will never reach greatness until you are willing to step out of the house.

POWER NUGGET #65: The belief we hold inside is a reflection of the life we'll live outside.

POWER NUGGET #66: Our emotions and our actions are tightly linked.

POWER NUGGET #67: Plant a seed today ... expect a harvest tomorrow!

POWER NUGGET #68: People are tremendous assets when you look for the best in them and commit yourself to helping them bring out that best.

POWER NUGGET #69: The gift of joy will come to you when you give the gift of yourself to someone else.

POWER NUGGET #70: A positive thinker is a person who always looks for the best in him/herself, all people, and in all situations. Thus, the positive thinker brings out the best in him/herself, all people, and in all situations.

POWER NUGGET #71: Champions are people who are willing to risk failure in order to succeed.

POWER NUGGET #72: Failure is not a bad thing; it is a stepping stone to success.

POWER NUGGET #73: Failure is a sign of great courage.

POWER NUGGET #74: Success is constantly improving to be your best where you are and with what you have.

POWER NUGGET #75: Success is a four letter word spelled — GROW!

POWER NUGGET #76: Love is a tiny word with huge assets.

POWER NUGGET #77: Men and women: Perfectly suited .. Explosively different!

SECTION THREE: Going All The Way

POWER NUGGET #78: Success is a journey that never rests.

POWER NUGGET #79: Man's approval means nothing unless you already have God's approval which means eternal life.

POWER NUGGET #80: Winning a game by cheating is not victory but losing in life.

POWER NUGGET #81: All people deserve respect as children of God.

POWER NUGGET #82: Is a champion someone who has never fallen? NO! The champion just keeps getting back up.

POWER NUGGET #83: Attack your enemies with LOVE!

POWER NUGGET #84: It takes more courage to be a man of peace than it does to be a man of war.

POWER NUGGET #85: A challenge is simply an opportunity in disguise.

POWER NUGGET #86: Attacking a person is judgmental; confronting a negative behavior is correction.

POWER NUGGET #87: The beginning of humanity is spelled — LOVE!

POWER NUGGET #88: Accountability is a blessing. It helps keep us on God's road. It is wise to have a friend or two who loves you enough to tell you what you need to hear, not necessarily what you want to hear.

POWER NUGGET #89: If you aren't connected with God, then you aren't connected with life.

POWER NUGGET #90: Determination is the power that keeps a dream alive.

POWER NUGGET #91: Being judgmental comes from a lack of trust.

POWER NUGGET #92: A friend is a special gift from God.

POWER NUGGET #93: Keep smiling, God is always with us.

POWER NUGGET #94: How can I feel better when I am depressed or frustrated? One way is to think about someone who is hurting more than I ... and figure out a way I can help that person.

POWER NUGGET #95: The marriage is the glue that binds the family together.

POWER NUGGET #96: The family is the glue that binds society together.

POWER NUGGET #97: I have a dream! My dream is alive! I will keep on keepin' on! I will not quit until the job is done!

POWER NUGGET #98: We can not truly help someone until we can move beyond sympathy to empathy.

POWER NUGGET #99: Congruency is the portrait of a champion.

POWER NUGGET #100: A champion is honest with him/herself and admits when he/she is scared, but then the champion goes forward and faces that fear.

POWER NUGGET #101: Faith is a power that is unseen but always is heard.

Conclusion

Suggested Reading

INTRODUCTION

What is a Power Nugget?

A Power Nugget is a thought or idea that God has inspired me with. When God gives me such a thought I write it down in what I call my Power Nugget Book. That little personal book has turned into this full fledged book you are about to read.

I am not sure I ever planned on publishing my Power Nugget Book. I know I didn't expect this to be my first book. But God had a different idea. He took this book and moved it up the priority list for my life. It is exciting to experience God in our lives.

Experiencing God is what this book is all about: experiencing His love, His touch, and His goodness in our lives. The book is linked together by three sections: A New Beginning, The Road That Leads To Success, and Going All The Way. These sections will lead you step by step to success. There are some similarities within each section. One reason for this is that success, like life, is a journey which has some constants along the road, such as faith, love, attitude, and hope.

Well, my friend, you are about to embark on what I hope will be an exciting adventure with God. My hope and prayer is that through this book God will use His hand to touch your heart, spirit, and your success. Enjoy the journey ... called life. God bless you!

MAKE IT A GREAT DAY!
Mark Bowser

SECTION ONE
A New Beginning

Have you ever wished you could have a do-over in life? That you could just start again. That you could stop the cameras by saying, "CUT! Stop rolling. Let's do that again. TAKE TWO: 'My Life.'" Wouldn't that be nice to be able to do that. Well, the truth is, we can start again. That is what this first section, "A New Beginning," is all about. Within this section you will discover the way to start over.

Some of you are pleased with your life and that's great. You are already successful but you need a new beginning for a new adventure. I believe you will also find this section very helpful.

Wherever you are right now is where you need to begin. So let's join together and take one step at a time with a new beginning.

POWER NUGGET #1:

In the beginning of time, God created the earth and along with it man and woman, and He bestowed greatness with each one, greatness unique to each individual which, if developed, will shape the world to righteousness.

I know something about you. I may not know you personally but I still know something about you. That something is this: YOU were born with the seeds of greatness and created by the Creator of the universe to be a champion. If you choose to tap into your greatness, then you will live an extraordinary life. We may not all be famous. We may not all be financially rich. But we all have greatness to make a difference in this world. Dr. Martin Luther King, Jr., said, "If a man is called to be a streetsweeper, he should sweep streets even as Michelangelo painted, or Beethoven composed music, or Shakespeare wrote poetry. He should sweep streets so well that all the hosts of heaven and earth will pause to say, here lived a great streetsweeper who did his job well."

History tells us a wonderful story about the greatness of individuals. It goes something like this. The year was 1815. The date was March first. This was the day that all of Europe will remember. It was as if all their nightmares were coming true. On that day, a small British ship sailed very quietly to dock on the French Riviera. A man stepped off the boat with a fire in his eyes. The man looked as if he were on a mission. All of Europe shivered at the thought of the return of this man. The nightmare was back. His name was Napoleon.

Napoleon had been exiled to the island of Elba, which is off the coast of Italy. During this period in his life, Napoleon didn't want to live and he attempted suicide. He carried a pouch around his neck which contained poison. He swallowed the poison but he did not die. He suffered cramps and convulsions and then he recovered.

Napoleon spent less than a year on Elba. He knew that the Allies had many differences and couldn't solve them at the Congress of Vienna. Napoleon hoped to exploit this weakness to regain what he thought was his right to power. After his recovery from the poison, Napoleon escaped from his British captors and stole one of their ships. Now he had just stepped off this stolen ship to begin his revenge on a frightened Europe.

The Allies immediately put their differences aside and joined forces to confront the tyrant. One of the men Europe looked to defend them against Napoleon was the Duke of Wellington. Wellington was a British hero determined to stop Napoleon. Wellington commanded the combined forces of Great Britain, Prussia, Belgium, and The Netherlands. A line was drawn in the sand and a battle was fought. That battle was to become one of the greatest military victories in all of history. The battle was called "The Battle of Waterloo."

Before the battle, Wellington was in Brussels preparing for his standoff with Napoleon. Accompanying the Duke was a member of the British Parliament named Thomas Creevey. As they were walking through Brussels Park they noticed a lonely British redcoat staring at a statue. Wellington grabbed Creevey by the arm and said, "There, look at him! It all depends on that article whether we do business or not. Give me enough of them and I am sure of victory."

On June 18, 1815, the line was drawn in the sand. Wellington had with him 67,661 men and 150 artillery guns. Napoleon had 71,947 men and 246 artillery guns. Because of heavy rain the night before, Napoleon chose to wait till close to noon to attack. This decision may have cost him the victory. The battle began at 11:25 in the morning and would last until 10:00 that evening. Napoleon pummelled the front of Wellington's line. Wellington's troops fought earnestly. Finally, all hope for victory was put on the British infantry. These solitary redcoats put together made an impressive stand. These boys stood their ground. They would not give up. They believed in their leaders. They believed in their cause. They began to believe in themselves. They did have greatness within them. The line in the sand stood and finally Marshal Gebhard von Blucher came and reinforced Wellington with his Prussian troops. Napoleon was forced from the battlefield licking his wounds. This battle finally closed the book on Napoleon's quest to rule Europe. Europe was safe again.

YOU, like the British redcoats, have greatness within you. Tap into your greatness and be the best YOU you can be!

POWER NUGGET #2:

Make sure what goes into your mind is positive because what comes out is always what went in.

Most of us have probably heard the statement "garbage in; garbage out." Well, that is a realistic representation of how our brains work. If we continually think depressing thoughts then we will begin to live a depressing life. But on the other hand, if we continually think happy, positive thoughts then we will live a happy, positive life. This is why it is vital that we pay attention to what we are putting into our brains. It is vital that we fill our brains with the good stuff of life. Begin reading good books. Begin watching moral entertainment. Begin focusing on what is positive, hopeful, and good. If we will do these things, then we will live a fulfilling, empowering life.

POWER NUGGET #3:

We are all beautiful in the eyes of God.

The late chaplain of the United States Senate, Peter Marshall, used to tell a story titled "The Keeper of the Spring," which I think illustrates beautifully how God looks at each one of us. The story is about a man who lived in a forest in the eastern Alps overlooking an Austrian village. This old man had been hired years ago by a wise town council to make sure the mountain waters flowed freely into the wonderful spring which flowed into the quaint village.

The old man faithfully year after year removed leaves, twigs, and everything which could contaminate or clog the flowing water. As a result, the village spring was an attraction for vacationers and swans alike. The village was peaceful, happy, and blessed.

One night years later another town council began talking about the almost mythical keeper of the spring. They wondered, "Why are we paying this man? Does anyone ever see him? This money could be used for better purposes." As a result, they decided to terminate the services of the old man.

For awhile, everything stayed the same. The spring was beautiful and the village blossomed. But then came autumn. The trees began to loose their grip on their leaves. Twigs and branches broke off the trees and fell into the stream.

One day, someone noticed something different about their wonderful spring. It was changing to a different color. Soon a haze came over parts of the spring and a sickening smell began to hover around it. The vacationers left the lovely village. The swans decided to look for a new home.

The town council called an emergency meeting. They realized what a terrible mistake they had made by firing the old man of the forest. They immediately hired him back. The old man got to work and performed the miracle again. Within a few weeks, the life-giving water was flowing freely and surely to the village spring. Soon all was normal, healthy, and blessed.

Many times we treat people in our lives much like the town council treated "the keeper of the spring." We appear to have no use for them and we take them for granted. But God looks at each of us much differently. He sees the beauty in each one of us. After all, He created us in His own image. When we look at people the way God sees them it puts a whole new light on them. Who knows? (God knows) ... there may be a "keeper of the spring" in your neighborhood.

POWER NUGGET #4:

Man must learn to crawl before he can walk and one must walk before he can run.

What would happen if a baby attempted to walk before it crawled? Most likely the baby would fall down, right? What would happen if someone attempted to perform brain surgery before he graduated from medical school? The patient would probably die.

Every goal has steps to reaching that goal. It is important not to skip too many steps. If you do, you are likely to stumble and fall. There are things we need to learn through the journey. There are things that have to be done before we can move forward. Success is a balance between patience and assertiveness. Find that balance and you will soon find yourself sprinting towards your goal.

POWER NUGGET #5:

Self-dignity and self-esteem are the greatest needs of every individual. Respect and love for oneself is vital for survival and a happy fulfilling life.

Gary Smalley and John Trent tell a wonderful story in their book *In Search of the Blessing*. The story is from the Civil War. One of the greatest heroes for the Union Army was General Chamberlain. He was very brave. He had nine horses shot from under him, was wounded many times, and was awarded the Medal of Honor. President Lincoln and General Grant respected Chamberlain very much so they chose him and his men to be the honor guard for Confederate General Lee's surrender at Appomatox Courthouse.

When the surrender was complete, General Lee began to ride down the road with Union soldiers standing on either side of him. The Union soldiers began to laugh and make fun of the enemy's leader. Chamberlain was not going to stand for this. He silenced his men and forced them to stand at attention, present arms, and salute General Lee as he made his way down the road.

Why did General Chamberlain force his men to do this? I believe it is because General Chamberlain understood the power of respect to an individual's self-esteem. General Lee deserved their respect. General Lee needed their respect. Their show of honor must have put a little joy into what was probably the worst day of General Lee's life. If we lose our self-respect then we lose who we are. General Chamberlain helped General Lee keep his self-respect. Now, my friend, let us go and do the same for someone in our lives.

POWER NUGGET #6:

Self-love is the kind of love that motivates a person to greatness.

Is it possible to love someone else if we do not love ourself? Jesus said we are to love our neighbor as ourself. What if we hate ourselves? Does this mean we should hate our neighbors? No, Jesus meant for us to love our neighbors with grace and servitude. Jesus also knows how hard this is to do if we have trouble loving ourselves. Jesus wants to give us a positive self-esteem which creates a healthy self-love.

How can we have this kind of self-love? I think the first step is to realize that we are a child of God. God loves us and we are created in His image. In fact He loves us so much that He sent His Son Jesus to die for us. Now, that is LOVE! Since God loves us so much maybe we could love ourselves too.

There is a great poem written by an unknown author that expresses the importance of self-love. It is titled "The Man in the Glass."

When you get what you want in your struggle
for self,
And the world makes you king for a day,
Just go to a mirror and look at yourself,
And see what that one has to say.

For it isn't your father or mother or mate,
Whose judgment upon you must pass;
The one whose verdict counts the most
    Is the one who you see in the glass.

When you get what you want in your
        struggle for self,
And the world makes you king for a day,
Just go to a mirror and look at yourself,
    And see what that one has to say.

For it isn't your father or mother or mate
Whose judgment upon you must pass;
The one whose verdict counts most in
        your life,
    Is the one staring back from the glass.

Some people may think you are a straight-
        shooting chum,
And call you a wonderful person
But the one in the glass says you're only
        a bum,
If you can't look yourself straight in the eye.

That's the one to please, never mind
        all the rest,

For you're with you clear up to the end,
And you have passed your most dangerous,
difficult test,
If the one in the glass is your friend.

You may fool the whole world down your
pathway of years,
And get pats on the back as you pass
But your final reward will be heartache
and tears,
If you've cheated the one in the glass.

Let Jesus Christ, the author and creator of all love, help you make friends with the "one in the glass."

POWER NUGGET #7:

When it is all said and done, at the heart of the champion is LOVE!

The nine fine-tuned athletes lined up at the starting line. This is what they had trained for. The race was the 100-yard dash. As the gun was raised, tension filled the air. BANG! The gun was fired. The athletes broke out in an awkward trot instead of a graceful gait. You see, this was the Seattle Special Olympics. Special was an understatement for this race of champions.

One of the contestants stumbled and fell to the ground. The young boy began to cry. The other eight athletes heard the cry in pain. They paused, turned around, and went to help their fallen comrade. One girl with Down Syndrome kissed the fallen athlete. She said, "This will make it better." They helped the little boy to his feet and they all joined arms and crossed the finish line together.

That is what being a champion is all about. The true victory in life is love.

POWER NUGGETS #8:

A man's actions choose his future.

The kind of life we will live is determined by the kind of day we choose to live. Mike Murdock says, "The secret of your future is hidden in your daily routine." Because of this it is vital that we consciously choose good habits.

There is a great story titled "The New Leaves." As the story goes, young Tommy was fast asleep when all of a sudden he heard a voice say, "Wake up!" Tommy woke up with a start and saw a little boy about his same age standing at the end of his bed. The boy was dressed in the whitest clothes Tommy had ever seen.

"Who are you?" asked a startled but not frightened Tommy.

"I'm the New Year," said the boy. "I've brought you your leaves."

"What leaves?" asked a bewildered Tommy.

"Your new ones, of course. My daddy tells me bad things about you."

"And just who is your daddy?"

"The old year, of course," said the boy. "He says that you are greedy and that you don't treat your sister very nice. He also said you threw your book in the fire. Tommy, all of this must stop."

A little fear began to creep into Tommy's mind as he said, "Oh, I must change, you say?"

The boy in white said, "If you don't change then day by day, year by year you will become worse and worse until you become a horrible man who has not a friend in the world. Do you want to be a horrible man, Tommy?"

A now very frightened Tommy sputtered out the word, "No."

"Then you must change today. Here, take your leaves." The boy handed Tommy what looked like white notebook paper. "Read one of these every day and soon you will be a nice boy."

On each sheet read little action steps like, "Help your mom and dad," "Be nice to your sister," and "Pick up your toys."

With that the New Year said, "Good-bye, Tommy. I will be back when I am old to see if you have been a good boy. Remember, bad boys make bad men and good boys make good men."

The New Year opened the window and was gone. The wind blew in the window and tossed the leaves out of Tommy's hand. "My leaves!" exclaimed Tommy. Tommy's mother came into the room to see what the commotion was about.

Tommy looked around the room for his leaves but he couldn't find even one. With confidence and conviction in his voice Tommy said, "Oh, well. But I can change without the leaves to remind me. I will not be a horrible man when I grow up." Tommy kept the promise to himself and he grew up to be a very fine man.

POWER NUGGET #9:

I have faith in Jesus Christ; therefore I am.

Have you ever heard the saying, "I think; therefore I am"? It is a good one and a true one but I think there is more to life than thinking. That something is faith. I am a Christian which means I believe Jesus Christ is the Son of God and died for my sins on a cross almost 2000 years ago. Faith is more important than thinking.

I grew up in the church and I was always taught at home and in church who Jesus Christ is and what He did to save me from my sins. Ever since I was a very little child, I have always believed in Jesus but I never knew what it meant to be a born again Christian until many, many years later. You see, even though I believed in Jesus, I always held a little of myself back just for me. Jesus wants us to surrender all of ourselves to Him. I had no problem with God having control of 95 percent of my life. I just wanted to maintain control of the remaining 5 percent. I soon discovered that that little 5 percent can and did get me in all kinds of trouble.

Things got so bad in my life that I felt they couldn't get any worse. I felt as if I had hit rock bottom. This was a good place for me because I saw only one direction to go and that was up. And when I looked up, I truly discovered Jesus Christ. On a December day in 1991 I made a decision. The most important decision I or anyone could make. I decided to follow Jesus. On that day I gave my life 100 percent to Him and I asked Him to forgive me of my sins and to come and live inside of me through His Holy Spirit and make me the champion He created me to be. And God has done all of that and much, much more. And since that day my life has been terrific. Now, I still have problems like everbody else but the difference is I now see the problems as challenges that God is solving and using to make me a better person.

I look back at that time of my life and don't recognize that person. I'm not the same person anymore. I regret the pain I caused in people's lives before I knew Jesus in an intimate way. I hope those people have forgiven me. Some of them I have not been able to personally express how sorry I am. I knew that my personal contact, even to ask their forgiveness, would have caused more pain in their lives. But there may be a day when they will allow me to approach them and express the love of Christ that is in me. It is possible that they may be reading this book. If that is so, then I ask your forgiveness. The guy you knew doesn't exist anymore. He's dead. I am a new creation in Christ. Jesus Christ has saved me and washed away my sins and my past.

Do you need Someone to wash away your sins like chalk from a chalkboard? That One is Jesus Christ. Where is your faith rooted? Have you ever thought about trusting Jesus? He is what life is all about. As the Bible says, Jesus is "... the way, the truth, and the life. And the only way to get to God."

POWER NUGGET #10:

A winner is not a perfect human being. There are no perfect human beings. A winner is an imperfect human being striving to be better.

Sometimes I can be a perfectionist. Because of this, I am sometimes too critical of myself and others. What I have to remind myself of is that we aren't perfect. Because of this fact, we will make mistakes. Sometimes they will be stupid mistakes. Well, that's part of life. When we make a mistake, we have to own up to it and then forgive ourselves. If the mistake can be fixed then fix it. If other people make a mistake then forgive them. Mistakes are part of life. When they happen, we need to look for the good in them. What can we learn? Where did we go wrong? How can I improve this situation? How can I show people I love them in spite of their imperfectness? Where do we go from here? These are the questions of a winner and you are a winner.

POWER NUGGET #11:

Patience is a weapon which can reveal miracles.

Patience is something with which I have difficulty. I am a go-getter who doesn't like to wait. But the truth is, we all need to learn patience. Through patience and persistence is usually how success happens.

During the reign of Queen Elizabeth, Dr. Thomas Cooper took on the tedious task of editing a known dictionary. He also improved it in other ways including adding thirty-three thousand words. Dr. Cooper had already been working on his project for eight years when his hateful, ignorant wife went into his library and burned every note he had on the project. She believed she was saving him from killing himself from too much study.

A short time later, Dr. Cooper went into his library and found the burnt mess. He inquired about who would cause such tragedy. His wife boldly and proudly said that she had done it. Dr. Cooper looked at his wife and said, "Oh, Dinah, you have just caused me a lot of trouble!" He then sat down and began another eight years of work to replace the notes she had destroyed.

Wow! Now that's patience. My friend, do you have that kind of patience? Do I? I don't know. I hope I would possess the same courage and conviction as Dr. Cooper to start again. Only with God is it possible for us to be like Dr. Cooper and live such patience, forgiveness, and persistence. I don't know about you my friend, but I am going to allow God to work His miracle in me.

POWER NUGGET #12:

PEACE — a calm emotion with tremendous strength.

Where does peace come from?

Norman Vincent Peale used to tell a story about a high steel worker by the name of Nick. They were building a stack, which was 600 feet in the air, up near Gary, Indiana. Now 600 feet is about 60 stories. One particular day, Nick was teamed up to work with a guy whose name he didn't know. All he knew was that the guy was called Preacher. Now Preacher was a very calm fellow. He never cussed or went out drinking with the other guys. Because of this, he was known as Preacher. Preacher was working on the high steel to earn money for a little church down south which was in debt. And on this day, Nick and Preacher were teamed up as partners.

Nick and Preacher were to work from inside a little trolley car that rode on the outside of the stack. It was moved up and down the stack by two little trolley wheels. They got up to about 500 feet when something out of the ordinary began to happen. There was the sound of fractured steel as one of the trolley wheels broke loose. The cage came crashing back against the stack. It was held up in the air only by the one remaining trolley wheel.

Finally, Nick and Preacher regained full consciousness and began to realize the situation they were in. Nick looked at Preacher and said, "If that other trolley wheel gives way we're goners!"

Preacher looked at Nick and said, "Don't worry, Nick. God will take care of you."

What did he mean, God would take care of him? Just in case Preacher didn't understand the situation they were in, Nick explained it to him again. He said, "Preacher, I don't think you get it. If that trolley wheel breaks loose were going to be killed."

With a small smile forming on his face, Preacher said to Nick, "Don't worry, Nick. Even so, God will take care of you."

That was when Nick saw for the first time in his life complete faith and confidence in Almighty God. Nick then realized that Preacher knew that even if that cage broke loose and came crashing down 500 feet to kill them, God would take care of them.

Well, the two men were rescued and it has been quite some time since that situation took place but Nick says that every time he goes through Gary, Indiana, and sees that stack shining brilliantly in the sky he thinks of that faithful day he learned to trust Almighty God.

PEACE — where does it come from? It comes from God.

POWER NUGGET #13:

Jesus said to me, "Mark, no matter how many times the crucifixion is replayed; there is always one conclusion — THE RESURRECTION!"

Many times God will speak to me through a thought. It usually is a very clear thought which is the answer to a problem I'm struggling with at the time. This was one of those thoughts.

I can sometimes be very hard on myself. I'll beat myself up over and over for past sins. I repent to God for the same thing many times. We only have to repent once. God forgives and forgets. The Bible says He separates us from our sin as far as the East is from the West.

This is what God was reminding me of through this Power Nugget. No matter how many times we read the story of Jesus's crucifixion, the conclusion is always the same — The Resurrection. He died for our sins and was done with it once and for all. He did not have to die over and over again. Once was enough. Jesus Christ finished the first time. When we truly repent (which means turning away from our sin) He forgives once and for all. That's why He is our Savior and Lord of all.

POWER NUGGET #14:

Everyone has a little child within him that needs to come out and play from time to time.

During a dinner party the host's children came into the dining room and began walking around the table completely naked. The hosts were so embarrassed that they continued talking as if nothing strange was happening. The guests obliged and followed suit. As the children left the dining room, there was a moment of silence around the table. One of the children was overheard saying, "See, I told you. It is vanishing cream."

Children have a way of bringing a spark to life. They are so simple, happy, honest, teachable, and curious. Just because we are adults doesn't mean we are to lose these qualities. I think these are some of the qualities Jesus was talking about when He told us to be childlike. As adults, we are to lose the foolishness of a child but hang onto the positive aspects of childhood. This will add tremendous spark and joy to your life.

There is a story of a mother firefly who was taking her children for a walk. As they approached a very dark woods the mother firefly said, "All right children, line up and do NOT shine your light no matter what happens. There are owls in here and if they see you they will swoop down and eat you."

Well, all the children lined up in a single file with the youngest at the end. After a little while, the mother firefly saw a light coming from behind her. She said, "STOP! Who lit their light?"

The youngest admitted, "I did, Mom."

"I told you not to. Why did you do it?"

The littlest firefly looked at his mother and said, "Well, Mom, when you gotta glow, you gotta glow."

Let your light so shine by taking on the positive qualities of childhood and let the child in you come out and play.

POWER NUGGET #15:

Happiness is always created from the inside, not from the outside.

Where does happiness come from? Is it given to us? Can we earn it? Happiness is given to us. It is ours for the asking. Happiness is a choice. We decide how happy or unhappy we will be. Wisconsin Odd Fellow wrote a poem titled "Happiness Is Within" which says, "It's not so much the world outside that makes us laugh or smile; it's more the thoughts within our hearts that make life seem worthwhile."

I know a story about an old wise man. This wise man lived in a small town. Every day this man would sit outside the local gas station and watch the cars go by. Every once in a while a car would stop and he would have the opportunity to talk with a neighbor or even a tourist passing through. On this particular day, the old man's granddaughter joined him at the gas station.

After some time, a car pulled up to the station. A man got out of the car and started to look around. The wise old man did not recognize the stranger and figured he was a tourist. The tourist came up to the older man and asked, "What kind of a town is this? Is it a nice place to live?"

The wise old man looked at the stranger and asked, "What kind of town are you from? Is it a nice place to live?"

The tourist said, "It's an awful town. Everyone is critical of each other and negative about the future. They gossip all the time too. I am glad to be leaving."

The old man said, "That's how it is in this town too."

After an hour or so, another car drove up. This time it was filled with a family of strangers. The mother jumped out in a hurry with two small children and asked where the restroom was. The old man pointed to a ragged, decrepit sign and the woman thanked him and hurried off with the children.

The father got out and walked up to the wise old man and his granddaughter. He asked, "What kind of town is this?"

The old man asked, "What kind of town are you from?"

The young father looked at the old man and said, "It's a great town. I wish we didn't have to leave. Everyone is very close. There is always a friendly hello and smile throughout the day. I feel we are leaving family."

"That is exactly like this town," said the old wise man.

After the nice little family had driven away the old man's granddaughter looked up at her grandfather with a puzzled look and said, "Grandpa, why did you tell the first man this was a terrible town and the second man it was a great town?"

The old man looked down at his beautiful little granddaughter and lovingly said, "Sweetheart, the truth is that people see exactly what they want to see. Our attitude is what makes the difference. The attitude we have determines whether it is an awful or marvelous place in which to live."

Well, there we have it. We choose whether we are going to live a happy or unhappy life. Abraham Lincoln said, "People are just about as happy as they make up their minds to be." Well, I don't know about you but I have made up my mind. I'm going to live a happy life!

POWER NUGGET #16:

Be happy where you are, but work towards the future.

Mary Sherman Hilbert shares the story about her neighbor, Ruth Peterson. When the stress of life seemed to be closing in on her, Ruth Peterson would go to her special place. Her special place was the beach. The sounds of the waves, the crisp clean air, and the signs of life always seemed to cheer her up. One day as Ruth was on her beach, a little girl was building something in the sand. The little girl saw Ruth and spoke, "Hello, I'm building."

"I can see that," said Ruth not really interested. She would have rather been left alone. "What are you building?"

"I don't know," said the little girl. "I just like the feel of the sand."

About that time a bird flew by. It was a sandpiper. "That's joy," said the girl.

"What do you mean?" asked Ruth.

"My mom says that sandpipers come to bring us joy."

Ruth desperately wanted to be left alone. She was depressed and felt smothered by the world. But the little girl wouldn't let up. "What is your name?" asked the girl.

"My name is Ruth Peterson."

"I'm six years old and my name is Wendy."

"Hello, Wendy."

As Ruth strolled away the little girl called to her, "Come back Mrs. P. and we will have another happy day." As much as Ruth hated to admit it to herself she felt better. Wendy had brought a little sunshine to her stormy day.

The next few weeks were very busy for Ruth and she didn't have time to go to the beach. One day, Ruth said to herself, "I could use a sandpiper." She grabbed her coat and went to the beach. She had forgotten about Wendy as she was walking on the beach. All of a sudden she heard, "Hi, Mrs. P. Do you want to play?" All Ruth needed was to have to deal with this little kid. Ruth had things on her mind and wanted to be left alone but being polite she asked, "What did you have in mind?"

"I don't care. What do you want to do?"

"How about charades?"

"I don't know what that is," said Wendy.

"Then why don't you just walk with me." As they were walking along Ruth asked Wendy where she lived. Wendy pointed to a home among a row of cottages. Ruth thought it a little strange to be living in a summer cottage during the winter.

"Where do you go to school?" asked a now curious Ruth.

"I don't go to school. Mommy says we are on vacation."

As Ruth said good-bye to Wendy to head for home, Wendy left Ruth with the same sunshine as before. Wendy had said it had been a happy day.

Three weeks went by and now tragedy had struck Ruth's family. Ruth's mother had died. In great distress, Ruth went to her beach.

She hoped she wouldn't have to deal with Wendy today. She didn't know if she had the strength. But as usual Wendy was there. Ruth said, "Please leave me alone today. I need to be alone."

"Why?" asked the puzzled child.

"Because my mother died."

"Then this is not a happy day. Did it hurt when she died?"

What a question! "Of course it hurt," said a shocked Ruth. Ruth did not understand Wendy's situation. She was too engulfed within herself to see Wendy's needs. Ruth walked off, leaving the little girl there on the beach.

The next time Ruth went to the beach Wendy wasn't there. Ruth thought this was strange and went up to the summer cottage and knocked on the door. A young woman, who appeared to have been going through her own tragedy, answered the door.

"Hi. I'm Ruth Peterson. I didn't see Wendy today and wondered where she was."

"Please come in," said Wendy's mother. "I'm sorry if Wendy has been bothering you."

"Oh, no. She is a wonderful child." Ruth discovered she truly enjoyed her times with Wendy.

"Wendy died last week. She had leukemia." A wave of despair struck Ruth. This unexpected news rocked her.

"Wendy enjoyed the beach," continued Wendy's mother. "When she asked to come here we couldn't disappoint her. She seemed to be healthier here. She wanted me to give you something, Mrs. Peterson." Wendy's mother went and got an envelope and handed it to Ruth. Inside was a drawing made with crayons. It was a picture of a beautiful beach, the glorious sea, and a bird. Underneath Wendy's masterpiece she had printed: "A sandpiper to bring you joy."

Ruth was overwhelmed with emotion. She and Wendy's mother spent the next few minutes crying together as they mourned for this special happy little girl named Wendy.

We can learn a lot from Wendy. She was a happy girl. Even through her pain, she was happy right where she was. I also believe she looked towards the future for what she called "happy days." We can be happy where we are. We can believe in a positive future. We can strive for that future. The result is a present, future, and memory of "happy days." As Almighty God spoke through the Apostle Paul, "I can do all things through Christ, because he gives me strength" (Philippians 4:13 NCV).

POWER NUGGET #17:

An idea is the greatest investment.

Not too many years ago when I was struggling in my life, I heard five powerful words spoken by motivational speaker Les Brown. The words he spoke touched my heart. His words were, "You've got greatness within you." Since the day I heard those words, it has been my understanding that one of the most powerful forces in the universe is a positive idea that is acted upon. I acted upon that idea and my life was ever changed for the better. Thanks, Les!

How about you? Do you have any good ideas stored in your brain that you never bothered to act upon? Well, I challenge you now to pull those ideas back out. Dust the cobwebs off the ideas and run with them. TAKE ACTION! You may discover your life is forever changed like mine. WOW! What an idea!

POWER NUGGET #18:

Motivation without direction is dangerous. Motivation with positive direction is success!

There is the story of an American soldier by the name of Murphy who was part of an American Tank Unit fighting with the British in the Libyan Campaign. The young G.I. soon found himself and his unit many, many miles deep into the desert. They went days without seeing any action. Boredom set in. One day, the commanding officer of this unit found this young man walking across the sands as if on a mission. The only problem was that the young American was wearing swimming trunks.

The commanding officer shouted, "Murphy! What on earth do you think you are doing and where are you going?"

"Well, sir," said Murphy. "It is such a nice day and I have a few hours off so I thought I would go for a swim."

"You must have been out in the sun too long. The ocean is 500 miles away."

"Boy!" said Murphy. "It's a beautifully large beach, isn't it, sir."

You see my friend, of all the problems Murphy may have had, motivation wasn't one of them. However, he did have a big problem when it came to direction. A friend of mine likes to say that you run into trouble when your mind gets idle. In our case (as well as Murphy's) that is true. My friend and I will find ourselves talking about all kinds of bizarre stuff when we have no direction for our motivation.

So, what's the answer? The answer is purpose. If you have a purpose for your life (not to mention your day or week) then your motivation will have a positive focus. And, positive focus plus motivation equals success. Later on in this book we are going to talk about how to obtain a positive focus through goals.

POWER NUGGET #19:

Hope is a little thing that carries big dividends in the journey of life.

Webster defines hope as, "A desire of some good, accompanied with a belief that it is attainable ..." The Bible talks about faith, hope, and love being of tremendous importance with love being the most important. As we can see, hope is a necessary ingredient to live an empowered life. When we believe something good is attainable we are more likely to take action to achieve it. Also, our thinking will be right. We will begin to visualize ourselves as successful. We will begin to believe in our dreams. We will begin to see the possibilities of those dreams realized.

POWER NUGGET #20:

Integrity and character go hand and hand.

There is a troubling trend flowing through our country. That trend is the idea that character isn't important. People have begun to believe that what they do in their personal life doesn't affect their professional life. Nothing can be further from the truth. If a man would abuse or lie to his wife and family then how could he be trusted in anything else? The answer is: HE COULDN'T!

Our character is important. It does mean something. Who we are goes with us no matter where we are.

An 1800's French statesman by the name of Alexander de Tocqueville made a study of American democracy. He wanted to discover what made America so special. This is what he found out as he so eloquently wrote in his piece titled "The Greatness of America."

"I sought for the greatness and genius of America in her commodious harbors and her ample rivers, and it was not there.

"I sought for the greatness and genius of America in her fertile fields and boundless forests, and it was not there.

"I sought for the greatness and genius of America in her rich mines and her vast world commerce, and it was not there.

"I sought for the greatness and genius of America in her public school system and her institutions of learning, and it was not there.

"I sought for the greatness and genius of America in her democratic congress and her matchless constitution, and it was not there.

"Not until I went into the churches of America and heard her pulpits flame with righteousness did I understand the secret of her genius and power.

"America is great because America is good, and if America ever ceases to be good, America will cease to be great."

Character does mean something. But don't worry if you aren't pleased with the character you are portraying today. You don't have to stay the way you are. Decide right this moment to begin living a life of integrity which means truthfulness, uprightness, and wholeness. Change what you believe and you will most certainly change who you are.

POWER NUGGETS #21:

Great strength comes from within, not from without.

The strength that carries us through life is not found in muscles of steel but in a muscle of the heart. Another way of explaining it is the spirit of a person. When a person gives his/her life to Jesus Christ then the Holy Spirit will come and live inside that person. The Holy Spirit is the strength inside a person. God, Jesus, and the Holy Spirit are the same. In fact, they are the three in One. So, it is Jesus that lives inside of us. With Jesus inside and beside us we have the strength to overcome life's struggles. The Bible promises us this in Philippians 4:13, "I can do all things through Christ, because he gives me strength" (New Century Version).

POWER NUGGET #22:

To me success is continually learning and growing and doing my very best always for Jesus Christ.

As I said before, I am a Christian. That means I have given my life to Jesus Christ. He is my Lord and Savior. My ultimate goal in life is to learn more about Him every day and grow closer to Him. I strive to do my very best in serving Him by following His example. I want to be more like Him every day of my life. He calls us to be our best.

Abraham Lincoln once took a sack of grain to a mill whose owner chose to live on a different path. This man was said to be the laziest man in Illinois. Abe watched the man for a while and then finally commented, "I can eat the grain as fast as you're grinding it."

The owner of the mill grunted and said, "Indeed; and how long do you think you could keep that up?"

Abe looked at the man and replied, "Until I starve to death."

We need to live the life that God has called us to live. That is a life of giving it our best in everything we do, at home, at work, and at play. What a wonderful way to live!

POWER NUGGET #23:

There is not coincidence with God.

Do things just happen? Are chance meetings believable? How about luck? Coincidence? I do not believe in these things. I believe that God has a plan for our lives. I believe that He arranges for us to be where we need to be and when. In my opinion, anything else would discredit Almighty God.

You might be thinking, "Mark, do you then believe that life is predetermined?" Yes. "Then is there such thing as free will?" Yes. "How can there be both?" That is a very good question. God created each one of us with a unique form of greatness, a greatness to accomplish His mission for our lives. As Mike Murdock expresses it, it is our job to discover what our life assignment is and then go out and do it. This is where the free will comes in. You see, we don't have to believe in God. We don't have to obey Him. We can live any kind of life we want to. It is absolutely our choice. We can either live inside His plan for our lives or outside His plan. If we choose not to obey Him then He will find someone who will. God's ultimate Plan will be done whether we play on His team or not.

I choose to play on God's team. It is the winning team (I've read the end of the book — Revelations). I choose to believe Jesus Christ. I know His plan for my life is the best plan. That's why I choose to follow and serve Him with my life. " 'I say this because

I know what I am planning for you,' says the Lord. 'I have good plans for you, not plans to hurt you. I will give you hope and a good future'" (Jeremiah 29:11 NCV).

POWER NUGGET #24:

Every day is your day ... and you've got what it takes!

Every morning when we get up we need to make a decision. That decision is that it is going to be a great day and we have everything we need to succeed today. Our attitude is a self-fulfilling prophecy. If we believe it, we can make it happen with God's help.

POWER NUGGET #25:

Leave it to God; He never fails.

Recently, a friend of mine named Tom gave me an article which was in *Guideposts*. The article is about a fellow Hoosier of tremendous faith. His name is Jonathan Byrd. Jonathan had a big dream. His goal was to build a huge cafeteria.

Jonathan loved to serve people. He delighted in watching people enjoy a good meal. He also was touched with the significance of how many important biblical events took place while people were eating together.

Jonathan dreamed of a cafeteria which offered at least 200 different items daily. The cafeteria would have a serving line almost 30 yards long.

People said it wouldn't work. They said it was doomed for failure. Why? They said it was because Jonathan planned never to sell liquor. Jonathan felt down deep in his heart that his decision was right. He believed it was what God wanted him to do.

Finally, the building process began in March of 1987. Nothing seemed to be going right for Jonathan. August of 1988 found Jonathan sitting dejected and depressed at a picnic table on the site of his drowning dream. They were $500,000 over budget and sinking fast. In the mist of all this, Jonathan never gave up on God. He believed in the Bible and knew God was the creator of all miracles.

Just then a miracle happened for Jonathan. It was a miracle of hope. Around that time a car pulled up at the site. Two couples got out of the car. One of the men was excitedly explaining the dream of Jonathan Byrd. The man was Dr. Gene Hood. Dr. Hood was a pastor of a Nazarene church in a nearby town.

Dr. Hood was thrilled when he saw Jonathan. He then noticed that his friend was depressed. He asked what was the matter. Jonathan said it was the worst day of his life. Dr. Hood then exclaimed to Jonathan, "Well, I'm excited about your plans. I can just see all the Southern Gospel singers in your banquet halls."

This is when God sent Jonathan's miracle. The Reverend Hood challenged Jonathan's faith. He said if Jonathan had enough faith to build this great restaurant, then he had enough faith to help him keep his banquet halls filled with some of the best Southern Gospel music Indiana had ever heard. Both men had enough faith.

Today Jonathan Byrd's cafeteria is a tremendous success in Greenwood, Indiana. Success through faith. My friend, we just have to turn our lives over to God. He has good planned for us. Good which is ours if we only believe. As it says in the Good Book, "... I tell you the truth, if your faith is as big as a mustard seed, you can say to this mountain, 'Move from here to there,' and it will move. All things will be possible for you" (Matthew 17:20 NCV).

POWER NUGGET #26:

True beauty is a reflection of who you are, not from what you do (as in job or career) or what you look like.

God tells us in His word, "It is not fancy hair, gold jewelry, or fine clothes that should make you beautiful. No, your beauty should come from within you — the beauty of a gentle and quiet spirit that will never be destroyed and is very precious to God" (1 Peter 3:3-4 NCV).

So, beauty comes from within. How do we have this inner beauty? By believing in Jesus Christ and allowing Him to live inside of us. When we let Jesus in our lives then He will soften and reshape our hearts to that "gentle and quiet spirit" that only He can give. Physical beauty is nice but without the true beauty inside the heart it is worthless. Let's all seek that inner beauty of God.

POWER NUGGET #27:

Curiosity is the uncovering mechanism to new discoveries.

What is it that motivates someone to face tremendous challenges to uncover the unknown? What is it that has made *Star Trek* so popular? Why has NASA sent probes to explore the planets? The answer is curiosity. The human being is a curious creature. We have a burning desire to know what is unknown. And it is this curiosity that brings about new discoveries, new inventions, new insights, and new benefits for the human race.

In May of 1803, the United States became twice as large when it purchased all of Louisiana from Napoleon. The cost of the land was $15 million which worked out to be around four cents an acre. Nobody knew exactly what was bought from Napoleon. What was on this land? Where did it lead? Was it a good buy?

Months before the land was purchased, President Jefferson had the wisdom to ask Congress for $2,500 to fund an expedition to explore the West. President Jefferson now chose Meriwether Lewis to lead an expedition. Lewis selected William Clark as his co-commander.

After 28 months of exploring the wild unknown, Lewis and Clark and their band of adventurers returned with only one casualty. It wasn't the rough terrain that killed this man. It wasn't the battles with Indians. It wasn't a wild creature like a grizzly bear or a mountain lion. It was an attack of appendicitis.

Overall, the journey was a tremendous success. The journals they kept and the specimens they collected were of unestimated value. Their curiosity flamed the adventuring spirit in America which urged her to push westward.

"Curiosity is the uncovering mechanism to new discoveries." What are you curious about? What unknown would you like to know? Well, the adventure is before you. All you have to do is start the journey. Take that first step today into a larger world.

POWER NUGGET #28:

The man is not the ship; the ship is the *man*.

Imagine you are the new captain of the United States aircraft carrier *The U.S.S. Enterprise*. You walk onto the bridge for the very first time. The ship has a tremendous reputation for excellence under her previous captain. Now that you are the captain, will that excellence continue without your doing anything? The answer is no. The ship does not set the standard; the captain does.

POWER NUGGET #29:

The ship does not make the man; the *man* makes the ship.

Just as with the aircraft carrier in the previous Power Nugget, the same is true for your business, your department, or your home. The object is nothing until it is shaped by an individual. When that happens, the object or community will begin to take upon it the reputation of its leader.

POWER NUGGET #30:

Commitment is a decision, not a happenstance.

One of my colleagues in the speaking industry, Zig Ziglar, likes to tell the story of a Catholic girl who started to date a Baptist boy. One day the girl came home love sick with joy. The girl's mother decided it was time to nip this relationship in the bud.

The mother told her daughter that Catholics don't marry Baptists. She explained that the differences would cause way too many challenges. But the girl refused to break up with the boy. She loved him and wanted to marry him.

Unable to convince her daughter, the mother went to plan B. Plan B was to convince the boy to take Catholic lessons. The daughter loved the idea and they approached the boy with the proposal. To their surprise, the boy accepted.

The engagement was announced and wedding plans were put in high gear. One day, the girl came home with tears flowing from her eyes. The girl said, "Mom, the wedding's off. Call the priest, cancel the church, and call the guests."

"What happened?" asked her puzzled mother. "Did he back out of the Catholic classes?"

"No, Mom. That's not the problem at all. He loves the classes. The problem is he has decided to become a priest."

You see, life is about commitment. And commitment is a decision. It just doesn't happen. We have many marriages ending today because couples say they have fallen out of love. I say that is a bunch of garbage. I question whether they were ever in love or know what love is, for that matter. Love is about commitment. Love is about hanging in there when times get tough. And believe me, every relationship has its ups and downs. But the commitment, THE VOWS, hold the marriage together through every storm. Commitment is the glue that bonds people together. Make sure you have this glue in your house.

POWER NUGGET #31:

Every sunrise is filled with the possibilities of a new day.

Just as the sun comes up every morning to sing forth a brand new day, every sunrise is an opportunity to start life fresh and new. The mistakes of yesterday are gone. Forgive yourself and start anew. We never know what exciting adventures are in store for us with each sunrise. There are two poems I would like to share with you which talk about starting life anew. The first poem was written by Whitman and the second by an unknown author.

"Finish each day and be done with it; you have done what you could. No doubt some blunders and absurdities crept in; forget them as quickly as you can. Tomorrow is a new day, you shall begin it well and serenely."

"I've shut the door on yesterday its sorrow and mistakes; and now I throw the key away to seek another room and furnish it with hope and smiles and every springtime bloom. I've shut the door on yesterday and thrown the key away. Tomorrow holds no fears for me, since I have found today."

Grab hold of the possibilities of a new day and *Carpe Diem* ... "Seize the Day!"

POWER NUGGET #32:

You can have tremendous health and energy ALL your life!

Is it truly possible for us to have tremendous health all our lives? The answer to this question is a resounding YES!!! The Bible tells us that "All things are possible for them that believe." The Bible also tells us that those who are in Christ Jesus have life.

The first step to living a life full of energy is to believe it is possible. BELIEVE ENERGY! Believe it is possible that you can get all your work done with energy to spare. Believe that you have reservoirs of energy that are ready to be used when you call on them.

After you begin to believe energy, the second step is to think energy. Never entertain a tired thought. For example, never say, "I just don't have the energy to make it through the day." Replace that kind of thought with "I feel good. I feel vibrant. God has blessed me with great energy."

Step three involves acting out energy. Famed American philosopher William James expressed a formula known as the "As if" principle. Using this formula you simply act as if you had energy. When you do this the emotion will certainly follow in time.

Step four involves taking care of your physical body. You need to eat healthy foods. You need to get on an exercise program. (Check with your doctor before starting an exercise program.) It is a good idea to take food supplements to support a healthy well-balanced diet. And we all need a certain amount of sleep. The brain needs sleep to replace certain chemicals in the brain. Also, a 15-20 minute power nap during the middle of the day can do wonders to refresh the body to conquer the rest of the day.

Well, you might be saying, "I agree with what you have said so far; but what about sickness and disease?" I have given a great deal of thought to this subject lately. As of the time of this writing, my father is having some prostate difficulty. They found cancer and will be removing his prostate in a few months. The "C" word can be very scary. Lately, I have been doing a great deal of research on healing. Let me share with you what I have discovered.

The Bible is packed full of people being healed of all kinds of sicknesses and diseases. In my search through the scriptures and other Christian material, one element has shined through like a beacon signaling a ship. That lighthouse is boldness of faith. Jesus Christ never gave illness a fighting chance. He commanded it to leave and it left and people were healed. He taught His deciples to do the same thing and they healed many people in Jesus' Name.

But why is there illness and disease in the world? Does it come from God? First of all, God hates illness and disease. It definitely does not come from Him. God allows sickness and disease. But why does God do that? Well, that is kind of a difficult question. You see, the Bible says that sickness and disease are curses of the law. In other words — sin. When sin came into the world, the world became imperfect and sickness and disease are part of that imperfect world. But can't God just fix it? Yes, God could fix it and some day He will when Jesus comes back. But why is He waiting? I am not sure I have an answer to that question. But I do know that the Bible says that Jesus won't come back until the gospel has been spread to every people group in the world.

If the Bible teaches about healing, is it applicable for us today? ABSOLUTELY!!! The Bible tells us so! "You know about Jesus from Nazareth, that God gave him the Holy Spirit and power. You know how Jesus went everywhere doing good and healing those who were ruled by the devil because God was with him"(Acts 10:38 New Century Version). But that was then, how about now? The Bible has the answer for that too. "Jesus Christ is the same yesterday, today, and forever" (Hebrews 13:8 NCV). The good news is that Jesus is always the same. He wants to heal us just like He did when He walked the earth. In fact, Jesus gives us the power to heal and be healed. He commands it. At the end of the Gospel of Mark, Jesus tells his followers (that includes us) to do certain things if we truly believe in Him. "Jesus said to his followers, 'Go everywhere in the world, and tell the Good News to everyone. Anyone who believes and is baptized will be saved, but anyone who does not believe will be punished. And those who believe will be able to do these things as proof: They will use my name to force out demons. They will speak in new languages. They will pick up snakes and drink poison without being hurt. They will touch the sick, and the sick will be healed' " (Mark 16:15-18 NCV). Jesus conquered sin and since He did that we have salvation by believing in Him. Since sickness is in the world because of sin then through Jesus we are healed if we believe. One thing I want to make very clear is that we are all sinners. We all need Jesus. But why do some Christians get sick while some unbelievers stay well? I don't know. Sometimes bad things happen to good people. But as the family of God, we can heal people in the Name of Jesus. The Bible says that we are to touch them with our hands and they will be healed. If we believe the person we touch will be healed and the person needing the healing believes he will be healed then he will be healed through our Lord Jesus Christ.

Jesus heals in a variety of ways. Sometimes the healing is instantaneous. Sometimes the healing takes time. Sometimes the healing comes through medical science. Sometimes the healing comes through the body's natural built-in healing processes. Sometimes the healing comes through a combination of these ways.

Let me toss a very difficult question into our discussion. Why do some strong believers in Jesus Christ not get healed? I am not sure exactly how to answer that question. I do know there comes a time in every Christian's life when God calls him/her home to Heaven. But remember, we do not know when that time is and until God calls us home we are to be His ambassadors here on earth.

I think there is another scripture that will be helpful to us as we discover how to conquer tough times. "Jesus answered, 'Have faith in God. I tell you the truth, you can say to this mountain, "Go, fall into the sea." And if you have no doubts in your mind and believe that what you say will happen, God will do it for you. So I tell you to believe that you have received the things you ask for in prayer, and God will give them to you' " (Mark 11:22-24 NCV). Notice that the Lord does not say that the mountain will disappear. He says it will move and believe me it WILL MOVE EVERY SINGLE TIME!!! This is what I have been taught. This is what I have learned. God gives us the amazing ability of turning tragedy into victory. Think about Christopher Reeve. He has suffered a tragedy in his life. Did God take away the paralyzation? No. Did the mountain move? YES!! Christopher Reeve is a great inspiration to many people of all walks of life. The courage God has given him is extraordinary. He is making a difference despite his injury. Will God someday heal Christopher Reeve so he can walk again? Quite possibly. But maybe Christopher is more effective in reaching this world the way he is. Only God knows for sure. We just have to trust Him and believe He has the best for us. After all He tells us, " 'I say this because I know what I am planning for you,' says the Lord. 'I have good plans for you, not plans to hurt you. I will give you hope and a good future' " (Jeremiah 29:11 NCV). We have to trust God, believe His words, believe in our and our loved one's healing, visualize the healing taking place, visualize the healing already accomplished and the individual in perfect health, and know God will turn everything to our good. As the Bible tells us, "All things are possible for them that believe," and "What is impossible with man is possible with God." JUST BELIEVE! I BELIEVE!

Ivan H. Hagedorn wrote an incredible story of healing titled "I Saw It Happen." The story is about the healing of sixteen-year-old Naomi Irene Crowley. Naomi began to have difficulty with her vision. The condition got so bad that in November of 1952 an operation was performed to restore the vision in her right eye and to correct the slant in her left eye. The operation appeared to be successful for a little while, but then Naomi lost all her eyesight in January 1953.

Naomi was wheeled into the operating room again. The hospital was to be Naomi's home for the next month. However, Naomi was not alone. Sharing her room was a kindly black woman named Mrs. John Carter. One day as Mrs. Carter sensed Naomi's darkness of mood as well as of sight, she said, "Naomi, there's a motto on the wall of this room, and it says 'The Lord is my Shepherd. I shall not want.'" Grabbing Naomi's hand, Mrs. Carter said, "You'll be all right, honey. You'll be all right. The Lord says He is your Shepherd and you shall not want — not even for your vision."

Naomi finally got to go home. Unfortunately, the surgery was only partially successful. Her sight in one eye was restored while the other eye remained completely blind. Naomi had to wear a black patch over her eye for two months. But Naomi's faith never wavered. She believed God would heal her eye. She knew she would see again.

Many people began praying for Naomi. Her fellow students at her high school lifted her up in prayer. A priest asked if he could bless her eyes. Naomi agreed. All these prayers and more were heard by God.

On Easter morning, Naomi felt like she was supposed to attend the Sunrise Service at her church. She knew it was God instructing her to go. The church was overflowing with people. It was a beautiful morning. The pastor (Ivan H. Hagedorn, author of this story) greeted the congregation cheerfully with the words, "The Lord is risen." The congregation responded with equal enthusiasm, "He is risen, indeed."

It had been a wonderful celebration of the risen Christ. It was one of those services you didn't want to end. Only God knew that the best was yet to come. As the recessional hymn was being sung, Naomi began to stagger and then fainted. The patch fell off of her eye. After a few moments Naomi regained her senses.

Naomi blinked her eyes. A miracle had taken place. Naomi could see. She could see with BOTH eyes. The chatter of voices enveloped the church as news of the healing was being spread. Finally, someone said in a whisper, "He is risen." Little by little, people joined the chorus and the congregation praised God by saying, "He is risen. He is risen, indeed."

God's healing power is truly amazing. Let me share with you a personal story of healing. I received a phone call early on a Sunday morning in November of 1994. The person on the other end of the line was an acquaintance of mine. He said, "Mark, there's been an accident." If you have ever been on the receiving end of words such as these then you know what it does to you. My stomach felt like it hit the floor. He then explained what had happened. A friend of mine had been in a bad accident. Her passenger had been killed instantly. My friend was lifelined to Methodist Hospital where she lay in a coma.

As I hung up the phone, a desperate feeling came over me. I didn't know what to do. But I knew I must do something. Out of desperation I started to pray. I discovered that was the best and most powerful thing I could do for my friend and all the families involved in this tragedy.

I then started to recruit other people to pray. I called friends. I called prayer lines. I called other ministries. Soon, we had prayer focused on Indianapolis from around the nation and beyond. I discovered later that I was not the only one recruiting a prayer army. In fact, prayer started almost immediately. People at the scene began the process by lifting up my friend in prayer. God answered these prayers.

My friend came out of the coma and was healed. She knows she is a walking miracle of God's love. The power of God's love is amazing. Do you or someone you know need healing? Maybe it is a physical illness or maybe it is a spiritual or emotional matter. God can touch you where you need it. Turn to Him. Allow His touch to work His miracles. Jesus truly "... is the same yesterday, today, and forever"(Hebrews 13:8).

P.S. I thought it appropiate to write a post script to this Power Nugget. It has been many months since I wrote the section you have just read. I am thrilled and blessed to announce to you that Jesus Christ has healed my dad. The healing did not happen the way we expected but God had bigger plans.

The original plan was to remove the prostate. They were not able to do this because they found cancer in at least one of the lymph nodes. When this happens, the prostate is not removed and they use other means to conquer the cancer. That other means was radiation.

The radiation therapy worked. All the cancer has been killed and my father still has a healthy, working prostate. GOD STILL WORKS MIRACLES! THANKS, LORD JESUS!

POWER NUGGET #33:

Each day is a new opportunity to succeed.

The great American, immortal Abraham Lincoln, once said, "The best thing about the future is that it comes only one day at a time." Each day brings with the sunshine new possible successes. It doesn't matter how great we were yesterday; we can strive to be better today. It doesn't matter how many failures we had today; we can be successful tomorrow. Each day is a new beginning. The slate is clean. Believe in the goodness of each day by believing the goodness of you!

POWER NUGGET #34:

The roadmap is the dream; the road is the goal; and putting it into action is the vehicle that makes it go.

It has been said that 90 percent of all people have no set goals; 5 percent of all people have set goals; and the remaining 5 percent of all people have set goals and write them down. My friend, we want to be part of that last category of people who have set goals and write them down. That is the group of people who are reaching their goals and living their dreams.

The Apostle Paul knew the importance of stretching to reach goals. He knew that goals helped us to become better people for Christ. Paul says, "I do not mean that I am already as God wants me to be. I have not yet reached that goal, but I continue trying to reach it and to make it mine. Christ wants me to do that, which is the reason he made me his. Brothers and sisters, I know that I have not yet reached that goal, but there is one thing I always do. Forgetting the past and straining toward what is ahead, I keep trying to reach the goal and get the prize for which God called me through Christ to the life above" (Philippians 3:12-14 NCV).

Goals keep us focused on a better tomorrow. That hope is a very important part of goal setting. Because without a goal to stretch you forward, many times the hope is not seen. Better tomorrows are in store for you. Those tomorrows start today with a goal. On the following pages I am going to show you my goal setting process.

Please take the necessary time to go through this process. Your future depends on it. The next few pages can be your map to a better future and a better you. Open the road map to your success by completing this process and live your dreams.

THE GOAL- SETTING PROCESS

STEP ONE: Pray

Pray to God asking Him for wisdom as you go through this process.

STEP TWO: A Mission Statement

A mission statement gives your life a direction. It is designed to be a life goal to focus everything you do. The mission statement is a few sentences that explain that purpose.

For example, here is my mission statement: "To give a lift to all I come in contact with. To bring hope to this world. To be the best communicator I can be to express Jesus' love the way He wants me to to everyone I have the blessing to meet whether it is in person, from the platform, on tape, or from the pages of a book. This is my life mission in the precious name of Jesus Christ."

By answering the following questions you will be able to focus your thoughts to create your mission statement.

WHAT'S IMPORTANT TO ME?

HOW CAN I MAKE A DIFFERENCE?

HOW DO I WANT TO BE REMEMBERED?

HOW DO I ACCOMPLISH THESE QUESTIONS?

Now take your above answers and create your mission statement.

MY MISSION STATEMENT:

STEP THREE: Brainstorming

The next step in the goal-setting process is to brainstorm in different areas of goals. There are four different areas of goals I want you too focus on: Personal Development Goals (spiritual/ growing closer to God, relationships, education, physical, etc...), Career Goals (dream job, financial, own business, etc...), R&R/ Fun Goals (vacations, sail around the world, movies, go to a ball game, etc...), Dreambuilding Goals (how you can give back: charities, big brother/sister programs, church, etc...) Use the space below to brainstorm in each category. Let your mind flow. Don't prejudge the goals you think of. Write down as many as you can.

PERSONAL DEVELOPMENT GOALS:

CAREER GOALS:

R&R/FUN GOALS:

DREAMBUILDING GOALS:

STEP FOUR: Ranking Goals

Now rank your top three goals in each category.

STEP FIVE: Working Goals

Now take your top two goals in each category plus two others from any of the categories for a total of ten working goals. List them on the next page.

1.   6.

2.   7.

3.   8.

4.   9.

5.   10.

STEP SIX: Why?

This is a very important step. The question is why must you accomplish the ten goals you have listed above? Your why must be bigger than your how.

STEP SEVEN: Setting Deadlines

Now set a deadline for achieving each of your ten goals. Remember, it is not so important that you reach your goal by the deadline date as it is that you reach your goal. The deadline date just gives you a target to shoot at. If you miss the target then just reload, aim, and shoot again.

STEP EIGHT: Visualization

Visualize yourself living your goals in their completed form. In your mind you have already accomplished your goals. It is done in the name of Jesus Christ!

STEP NINE: Action Steps

Now think of three action steps you can take for each of your ten goals. TAKE ACTION NOW!

STEP TEN: Praise God

Pray to God thanking Him for helping you with this process. Thank Him for your new goals. Thank Him in advance for achieving them. Thank Him for your better tomorrows and a better you.

Congratulations! You have just completed a process most people will never go through. You are in the elite group of not just goal setters but goal achievers. Go through this process at least once a year or whenever you run out of goals to achieve. Every day is your day and you've got what it takes. GO FOR IT!

POWER NUGGET #35:

It is not as important WHERE you are going as it is WHY you are going there. The why has got to lead the where.

It was William Shakespeare who said, "Strong reasons make strong actions." In the goal-setting section we discussed a little about the WHY. If your reasons for accomplishing something are big enough then you will automatically figure out how to accomplish it. The WHY has to create a MUST! When your reasons turn desire into a must then you are already well on your way to success. Your attitude becomes I must accomplish this because.... The next thing you know is that you are running towards your goal. This is the formula of the champion and YOU are a champion.

POWER NUGGET #36:

To live an empowered life, character is a requirement, not a choice.

It has been expressed that character is doing the right thing when nobody is watching. Many, many years ago in ancient Greece, an old sculptor worked hard on a piece of stone. He took much care as he chiseled a little at a time. The sculptor was careful to make every detail as perfect as possible. When finished, this piece of stone would sit high above on top of a shaft and would become the top part of a column. The column in turn would help support the roof of the temple.

A government official was walking by and noticed what the sculptor was doing and asked, "Why spend so much time on that section? It will be fifty feet in the air. No one will be able to see those details."

The old, wise sculptor looked at the man and said, "God will see it."

Character is a must for your life. In fact, that is what life is about. It was Samuel Johnson who said, "Life, like every other blessing, derives its value from its use alone. Not for itself, but for a nobler end the eternal gave it; and that end is virtue."

SECTION TWO
The Road That Leads To Success

If you were planning a car trip from Chicago to Washington, D.C., what is the first thing you would do? Probably get a map and find out what roads to travel on. Right? Well, success is the same way. This next section, "The Road That Leads To Success," can not only serve as your roadmap pointing you in the right direction but it can also put you on the road itself. So, buckle your seat belt and get ready to drive on the road of success.

POWER NUGGET #37:

Help someone love him/herself and you have made a friend for life.

Self love is one of the basics of life. Unfortunately, there are many people who are lacking this fundamental element of life. They have a low self esteem which plagues their day with loneliness, depression, and doubt. They can be in a room full of people and feel completely alone. On the other hand, people who believe in themselves can be by themselves and not feel alone but perfect contentment.

Dr. Norman Vincent Peale said, "Think positively about yourself, keep your thoughts and your actions clean, ask God who made you to keep on remaking you." God is the perfect sculptor. He chisels away the rough edges of our lives (if we allow Him to).

The best gift we can give to others is to help them believe in themselves. Dr. Peale also said, "Believe you are defeated, believe it long enough, and it is likely to become a fact." Part of being a friend is helping others drop self doubt and believe in the goodness that God has put into them. If you do that, that person will begin to see the light instead of darkness and you have made a friend for life.

POWER NUGGET #38:

FAITH — The great motivation!

A friend of mine told me a story that goes something like this. The story is about a boy who wanted a red bike. The little boy knelt beside his bed and began to pray, "God, if You give me a red bike then I'll be good for the rest of my life." The boy thought about that for a moment and then decided he couldn't do that so he changed his prayer and he said, "God, if You give me a red bike then I'll be good for three months." Well, he thought about that for a moment and figured that he couldn't do that either so he changed his prayer again. The little boy said, "God, if You give me a red bike then I'll be good tomorrow." The boy was contemplating amending his prayer again when out of the corner of his eye he saw a small statue of the Virgin Mary sitting on his dresser. He grabbed the statue, wrapped it in a towel, and tossed it under his bed. He then looked up to Heaven and said, "All right, God, I've got your mother and if You ever want to see her alive again then You'll give me a red bike.

Well, whether we agree with his motives or not, we have to agree the kid was motivated. But how are we motivated? We are motivated a few different ways. One of those ways is through our faith. If God can get us to believe then He can motivate us to take certain actions. But how can we believe and conquer doubt? By getting into the word of God. We need to fill our minds with God's thoughts. We are blessed with the opportunity to read the inerrant word of God called the Holy Bible. The more we read the more we will believe. Let's get motivated and read, read, read!

POWER NUGGET #39:

Boldness of faith conquers all defeat.

A huge drought had devastated a small farming community. This particular community was deeply rooted in religious faith. The local preacher set a day and time when the community would come together at the edge of one of the fields to pray for rain. On that day, a large crowd gathered together. The preacher climbed up on a bale of hay and looked over the congregation. He then said, "Brothers and sisters, we have come together to pray for rain."

A big "Amen!" came from the crowd.

The preacher with all seriousness asked his congregation, "But do you have enough faith?"

"Amen! Amen!" shouted the excited crowd.

"Then," continued the preacher. "I have a question for you." A hush went over the crowd. The preacher asked, "If you have enough faith then where are all your umbrellas?"

FAITH. Do you have enough faith? Faith creates miracles where tragedy reigned. There is a wonderful story in the Bible about Jesus and His disciples. It had been a long day of preaching and healing people when Jesus and His disciples got into a boat.

As they were out to sea, a storm appeared. The waves rocked the little boat. Water gushed over the sides flooding the boat. The disciples were terrified. They looked for the Master. Where was

He? They found Jesus fast asleep in one end of the boat. What was the Master doing? Didn't He care if they died?

They woke Jesus up and cried, "Master, we are dying. Don't You care?"

Jesus slowly stood up and commanded the sea and storm, "PEACE, BE STILL!" Suddenly there was a great calm on the sea. The disciples were amazed that even the sea obeyed His commands. Jesus marveled at the unbelief of His followers.

How strong is your faith? Jesus said that if we have as much faith as a mustard seed then all things would be possible for us (see Matthew 17:20). Build your faith by building your time with Jesus Christ. Get to know Him and you will get to know great faith.

POWER NUGGET #40:

See the opportunities! Sieze the opportunities!

Many people go through life and do not see the positive possibilities around them. Others see the possibilities but never act on them. My friend, the only way to succeed in life is to first see the possibilities and then seize them by harnessing the courage to act on them.

I know a great poem written by an unknown author which speaks to this truth. It is titled "It Can Be Done."

Somebody said that it couldn't be done,
*   But they with a chuckle replied,*
That "maybe it couldn't" but they would be the ones
*   Who wouldn't say so till they'd tried.*
So they buckled right in with a trace of a grin
*   On their face. If they worried, they hid it.*
They started to sing as they tackled the thing
*   That couldn't be done. And they did it.*

Somebody scoffed, "Oh you'll never do that,
*   At least no one ever has done it."*
But they took off their coats and took off their hats
*   And the first thing they knew they'd begun it;*

With the lift of their chins and a bit of a grin,
If any doubt rose they forbid it;
They started to sing as they tackled the thing
That couldn't be done, and they did it.

There are thousands to tell you it cannot be done,
There are thousands to prophesy failure;
There are thousands to point out to you, one by one,
The dangers that wait to assail you,
But just buckle right in with a bit of a grin,
Just start in to sing as you tackle the thing
That cannot be done, and you'll do it.

You have what it takes. This is your day. See those positive possibilities around you and seize them by taking action. GO FOR IT!

POWER NUGGET #41:

Focused concentration creates breakthroughs in your life.

A few years ago, I had so many things going on in my life that I discovered I was not able to give my best to any of them. They were all worthwhile things; I just could not do everything. I had to start prioritizing my life. Great progress was made when I started to focus my time and energy on a few selected opportunities.

Even today, I have to be careful I don't overload myself with things to do. Life is a balance and success is found in that balance. Where are your priorities? When you discover your priorities, then you will discover your balance and success.

POWER NUGGET #42:

Believe and succeed!

One of the most powerful techniques for reaching your dreams is known as positive imaging or positive visualization. This is how it works. You visualize your goals and dreams in their perfected form as if you have already achieved them. This technique helps bring into your life the actualization of those dreams.

Why does positive imaging work? Positive imaging works for three reasons. One, what we focus on most will draw us toward it. In other words, the things we think about most will ultimately influence us to take actions toward those things. Two, our minds can't distinguish between reality and an imagined reality. Three, it has been proven scientifically that by using positive imaging the same portion of the brain is stimulated as if you were actually participating in that event. This is very powerful. A person can gain valuable experience for an event through positive imaging.

Dr. Norman Vincent Peale has written a tremendous book titled *Positive Imaging*. In this book, he tells a story of a young boy who discovered himself and his potential through positive imaging.

This little boy grew up in Cincinnati, Ohio. It was a very cold winter morning and young Roger was walking down the street. He came upon a huge building which had a large plate glass window facing the street.

Roger peered through the window. He was fascinated at all the activity going on inside this building. This building was the home of that great newspaper *The Cincinnati Enquirer*.

Just then, a big rough-looking man caught the young boy's attention. The man was sitting behind a desk in the center of the room. The desk had papers scattered all over it. Papers were even on the floor. They were editorials for the newspaper. The man wore a green visor which was shading his eyes from the bare lightbulb hanging above his head. He had an ugly unlit cigar sticking out from between two withered-looking lips. Somehow, Roger knew this man was in charge of what seemed to be chaos going on inside this building.

About that time, a police officer was strolling past Roger. Roger excitedly called out, "Officer, officer! Who is that man in there ... the one with the cigar and the visor?"

The officer humored the young boy. "Him? That is the editor of *The Cincinnati Enquirer*."

The boy was transfixed by this editor. He watched this man intently for quite a long time. Finally, Roger went on his way. He looked exactly as he did before but somehow he was different. He didn't notice the cold anymore which had previously been ripping through his tattered hand-me-down clothes. He had a vision going through his mind. The vision was a replica of what he had just seen back in that window but with an important change. It was thirty years in the future and he was the man sitting in the editor's chair.

That evening, Roger prayed to God to help him reach his dream. He then visualized his dream again. He did this night after night after night combining positive prayer with positive imaging. By doing this with God's help, Roger released tremendous power and focus into his life. As a result, Roger reached his dream. You see, Roger Ferger not only became the editor of *The Cincinnati Enquirer*, he became its publisher and owner too.

Positive Imaging is a tremendous exercise of faith that has the mysterious power of helping you reach your dreams. I can not think of a situation in life where positive imaging would not help. Try it! I am confident you will become a believer in this exercise as well.

POWER NUGGETS #43:

Believe in yourself and people will begin to believe in you too.

There were parts of his job that Sheriff John Charles Olsen simply hated. Today, he had to perform one of those dreaded tasks. Today, he had to evict a father and three children from their home. To make things worse, it was a week before Christmas.

Now, how did this ugly situation come about? Stephen Reade had been a successful salesman in New York City. So successful that he was able to support a wife and three children. Tragedy then struck the Reade family. Stephen's wife took sick and died. Before she died, she made Stephen promise to take the children to live in the country. She had grown up in the country and she thought city life was what made her sick.

Stephen, being an honorable man, took his promise to his wife seriously. He packed up the kids and moved to the country. Stephen rented a farm from Mr. Sam Merske. As you probably have guessed, Stephen took to farming like a fish takes to breathing air. He was a terrible farmer. As a result, he couldn't pay his rent. Mr. Merske was quite patient with Stephen but eventually the inevitable had to be done. Now it was Sheriff Olsen's job to carry out that task.

When Sheriff Olsen got to the Reade house he found that the only ones home were the three Reade children. They invited the Sheriff in to wait for their father. After quite some time the sheriff became restless. Ellen asked the Sheriff if he was restless.

"Kinda," said the Sheriff.

"I am supposed to give you a letter when you get restless." Ellen went and got a letter and handed it to the Sheriff.

Sheriff Olsen worriedly opened the letter and began to read it to himself. It was from Stephen Reade. It was awful. He was giving his children away. This was supposed to be his Christmas gift to them. He thought they would be better off with adopted parents who could take better care of them.

The Sheriff quickly packed up the Reade children and took them to his house for his wife to watch over. The Sheriff then went in search of Stephen Reade. He found him trying to leave town on a freight train. Sheriff Olsen grabbed Reade and dragged him off the train and put him in his car.

After a while, Stephen pleaded with the Sheriff to let him go. He said he was no good for his children. He said he had lost his nerve and was scared. The Sheriff looked at Stephen and said, "Do you think I don't know what scared is like? Today, I have to dress up like Santa Claus and pass out Christmas presents to the children. Now that scares me. That makes me very uncomfortable."

Stephen Reade grunted. "Oh, you think it is so easy?" asked the Sheriff. "If it is so easy then you do it. I'll make a deal with you. If you play Santa Claus for me then I'll get you a job. Besides, my wife is bringing your kids and I am sure they will get a kick out of seeing their father play Santa Claus."

A short time later they had Stephen Reade dressed up and on stage as Santa Claus. He was the most depressing looking Santa

Claus ever. His head was down and it looked like he didn't have a friend in the world. The Sheriff wondered if he had made a mistake by putting Reade up there. He had hoped it would give him confidence again. Then, things got worse. Sam Merske sat down beside the Sheriff and Merske was hopping mad. Most of the presents had been bought at Merske's Dry Goods Store and all the presents were wrapped in Merske's paper because he was the chairman of the celebration committee. Merske had a lot riding on the celebration. "You have your nerve sitting here," said Merske to the Sheriff. "Who do you have up there in those whiskers?"

Little Ellen Reade who was sitting next to the Sheriff said, "It's my father, Mr. Merske. Isn't he wonderful!"

Sam Merske said to the Sheriff, "So, you put that no good bum Stephen Reade in that suit. That's just wonderful. I'll get you for this, Sheriff."

Stephen Reade began handing out the presents to the children. As always, there were two, three or even four children who were unhappy with their presents. Because of this the committee always kept a few extra presents for these children. The only problem was the Sheriff forgot to tell Reade about the extras.

Oh, no! Here came Johnny Pilshek and he was mad. He had gotten mittens and he didn't feel that was an appropriate gift at all. He marched up to Santa and said, "I don't want mittens. Mittens aren't a real present."

"You are right, Johnny. Most mittens aren't a real present. But these are special mittens. The label says they are made of interwoven, reprocessed wool. We had to order them specially for you at my home in the North Pole."

"But I already have mittens," said Johnny.

Santa, I mean Reade, took Johnny's hand in his and inspected it. He then said, "I know you have mittens but you need these special ones. You have very special hands, Johnny. You need to keep those fingers of yours nimble. If a baseball player at your age gets frozen fingers he will spend his whole career in the minor leagues. And, Johnny, we don't want you anywhere but the major leagues."

At that moment, Johnny had a new perspective on the mittens and his future. Johnny went away dreaming about baseball and the major leagues.

Just then little April came forward. She said, "I think there has been a mistake. This present was meant for a boy."

"We don't make many mistakes," said Reade. "But let me see what we have here." Reade examined the package and it was a drab grey muffler.

"I don't mind it being a muffler but this one was meant for a boy," said April.

"Well, you are right, April. This muffler was made for a boy and I know it is ugly but we chose this especially for you. You are a very pretty girl, April, and you are going to get even prettier. But the truth is you have to protect your voice. To get on television or in the movies you have to have a good voice."

"Do I have to wear it all the time, Santa?"

"No, just when it gets below freezing. You have your mother check the thermometer before you go out and if it is below 32 degrees then you wear it."

"Yes, Santa, I will. Thank you!"

And so it went that on that day all the children were happy. Sam Merske said to the Sheriff, "Pretty tricky. Having Reade put on an exhibition for me of his sales skills. All right. I will give him a job."

The Sheriff was shocked. That was not his plan at all. Things were turning out better than he expected. Now it felt like Christmas. Just then, the piano was beginning "Jingle Bells." Sheriff Olsen joined in with the singing with a joy he had never sung with before.

The moral of the story is believe in yourself if you want others to believe in you, too. And the truth is we should believe in ourselves. For remember, you and I are children of the living God.

POWER NUGGET #44:

If you can't see the light at the end of the tunnel then light a match and create your own light with God's help.

Many times we look at the darkness and despair in our lives as an impossible mountain to surpass. But just like the great mountain climbers, the mountain is conquered one step at a time. Light that match, my friend, and take that first step of faith.

POWER NUGGET #45:

When you help others shoot for the moon you will then find yourself among the stars.

There is a biblical law that says that if you give it will be given to you. By the same law, if we help others then we ourselves will be helped. What I mean by "help others shoot for the moon" is to become a Dream Builder. A Dream Builder is someone who helps another live his/her dreams.

Do you know someone who could use a helping hand? Do you know someone who is pursuing a dream? Is there some way you can be a Dream Builder for this person? Yes, you say? Great! Now go build some dreams. What if your answer was no? Are you sure you can't help? How about prayer? Prayer is the most powerful thing we can do. Prayer is the weapon of the Dream Builder. We all can pray so we all can be Dream Builders.

POWER NUGGET #46:

Be a dreamer and an achiever.

I once heard an audio autobiography of a great man by the name of Lee Iacocca. Lee Iacocca is one of America's premiere business leaders of all time. Why? Was he lucky? Of course we know the answers to these questions is no. Lee Iacocca is a champion who had the courage to stare adversity in the face until the victory was secure.

Lee grew up during the Great Depression in Allentown, Pennsylvania. At age fifteen, Lee caught the deadly sickness, rheumatic fever. Since the cure included lots of rest, Lee found he had tremendous amounts of time on his hands. To pass the time, Lee began reading books and he developed a passion for excellence. This is a quality Lee would soon discover would pay off nicely in his future.

After Lee had graduated high school, he attended a tough engineering school. He loved it. It was a disciplined atmosphere in which Lee thrived.

During his college years, Lee drove a 1938 Ford automobile. It was a car which had seen better days. Lee joked with his friends, "Those guys need me. Anybody who builds a car this bad can use some help."

Lee received his masters degree from Princeton and in 1946 entered Ford's extensive training program. This program covered the entire making of a car from beginning to end.

After a short time, Lee discovered his love was for people and not machines. He decided to start over again in a low level sales position at Ford's district office in Pennsylvania. Lee's enthusiasm shot him up the ranks in a hurry. Lee learned the fine art of listening. He found that one must compromise to hack out a solution. Great listening skills were a great asset for Lee in every area of his life from personal to professional. The key was to listen and really hear what people were saying even if he disagreed with them.

In 1956, sales at Ford Motor Company were dismal and Lee's district in Philadelphia was the poorest of the poor. But Lee stubbornly looked for the positive light at the end of the tunnel. He found that light with an idea. Lee came up with a plan for long-term financing. It was a huge success. It was a 36 month payment plan of $56 a month. The plan was christened 56 ($) for 56 (1956). Their sales district went from worst in the nation to number one in a month's time. Ford was so impressed they made Lee's idea a national program.

Lee was offered a job at the company headquarters and within four years he became vice president and general manager of Ford Division. Lee then helped develop a car known as "the Mustang." It was a hard sell but Lee and his team pushed it through and on Friday, April 17, 1964, the Mustang hit the market. The Mustang was a HUGE success! In its first two years, the Mustang netted profits over one billion dollars. Lee became a national hero. He and the Mustang appeared on the covers of both *Time* and *Newsweek*.

On December 10, 1970, 45-year-old Lee Iacocca became president of Ford Motor Company. This was an exciting time for the Iacocca family. Little did they know that less then eight years in the future Lee would be out of a job.

On July 13, 1978, an insecure second grandson of the founder of the company, by the same name of Henry Ford, fired Lee. The firing came as a complete surprise and with no seeable reason. To this day, Lee doesn't know why he was fired. The humiliation for Lee was overbearing. Lee said the toughest part for him was the embarrassment he felt towards his family. He also felt very abandoned. Not one of his friends from Ford dropped a note or gave him a call. Lee never did understand that.

It didn't take long for the offers to pour in. Lee was a great leader and many, many companies wanted him. But the only industry Lee was interested in was automobiles. It was in his blood.

Chrysler Corporation was in bad shape and they wanted Lee. Lee took the challenge and immediately set about a massive reconstruction of the company. He did it quickly and effectively.

At this time, the nation was in a great recession which cut business in half. This made Lee's job much tougher than it already was but as Dr. Robert Schuller has said, "Tough times never last but tough people do." Lee did exactly that. He got tough!

He went to the United States government and asked them for a loan of one billion two hundred million dollars. Lee convinced the Congress to back his loan. He told them that if Chrysler were to fail the American taxpayer would have to pay $2.7 billion in taxes to fulfill the Chrysler pension payments. Lee told them that they could either loan him $1.2 billion now and hope he paid it back or pay $2.7 billion later with no reimbursement. The vote in the Congress was a landslide in Chrysler's favor.

Next, Lee went to the company. The workers would have to be convinced to take a cut in pay. Lee shocked everybody when he cut his own salary to only one dollar a year. Now that's a champion example! Chrysler then had to gain the public's confidence. Lee instituted an advertisement campaign to accomplish just that. It worked! Lee promised the consumer excellence and that is what they got. The excellence that brought Chrysler back was called "the K car." It was a phenomenal success. Chrysler was back!

On July 13, 1983, Chrysler shocked the nation when they paid back their government loan SEVEN YEARS EARLY! WOW! Chrysler is strong because of championship leadership of a man named Lee Iacocca.

You are a champion too. BE A DREAMER AND AN ACHIEVER! Will there be tough times? Yes! Will there be failures? Yes! But if you keep on dreaming and striving for success, then like Lee your dreams will come true. Just follow the words of Walt Disney when he said, "All our dreams can come true — if we have the courage to pursue them."

POWER NUGGET #47:

When things seem at their worst then REJOICE because there is only one direction to go — UP!

Recently, the youth pastor at my church, Curt Walters, told our youth group a story. It was a story of a boy nicknamed Sparky. Sparky had a rough childhood. He was one of those kids who didn't have many friends. It wasn't that people didn't like him; it was just that people didn't notice him. Sparky was one of those kids that faded into the background.

Sparky had great difficulty with his schoolwork. When he was in the eighth grade he failed every subject. His high school years weren't much better. He still holds the unprestigeous record for being the worst physics student in school history.

As you can imagine, all this rejection gave Sparky a self-confidence problem. He refused even to ask a girl for a date for fear of being rejected.

However, Sparky did discover he had a talent. He was an artist. He loved to draw his own cartoons. Soon a dream was formulated in Sparky's heart and mind. He desperately wanted to be an artist for Walt Disney.

After graduating from high school, Sparky wrote a letter to Walt Disney Studios inquiring about a job. He received a form letter asking him to draw a funny cartoon of "a man repairing a clock by shoveling the springs and gears back inside it."

Well, Sparky finished his assignment and sent it back to Disney along with some of his other work. After an agonizing wait, Sparky received a letter from Disney. It was another form letter informing him that they didn't have a job for him. REJECTION AGAIN! Could it get any worse? What did life have in store for a kid like Sparky?

Sparky continued to draw despite his setbacks. He decided to tell his life story through a cartoon. He drew a cartoon of a little boy who was the ultimate loser. A little boy who fell down time and again trying to kick a football. A little boy who picked out a Christmas tree which made a flag pole look glamorous. A little boy who lost baseball game after baseball game.

If you haven't guessed it, that cartoon character has become one of the world's most loved characters — Charlie Brown. And the creator of this cartoon strip *Peanuts* was none other than Charles "Sparky" Schulz.

Just as with the life of Charles Schulz, God has a plan for each of us. Sometimes life is tough. Sometimes we have trouble seeing the mountain because we are still bogged down in the valley. No matter how bad things may seem we must continue to look up. God can transform our lives in an instant. We must trust in Him and continue to work for our dreams. We truly can "... do all things through Christ, because He gives me strength" (Philippians 4.13 NCV).

POWER NUGGET #48:

The most powerful thing in the universe: A positive idea that is acted upon.

Have you ever had a great idea that you knew for sure would make you a million dollars? The answer is probably yes. Where is your million dollars? Probably not in your bank. Why? Because action was not taken. Most ideas that flow in our brains lay dormant because we don't act upon them. My friend, the next time a great idea comes in your mind make sure you take action. GREAT IDEAS + ACTION = SUCCESS!

POWER NUGGET #49:

JESUS CHRIST — The Great Dreamer!

God had a dream. His dream was to be our friend. But sin came into the world and made that seem impossible. You see, God is righteousness and truth. Sin made us evil and corrupt. Sin became a barrier between us and the Creator of the universe.

God had a plan to fulfill His dream. God does not believe in impossibilities. For the Bible says that what is impossible with us is possible with God. So God sent His only Son Jesus Christ to bridge the chasm between Himself and us. Jesus went to a cross and became sin for us. He took upon himself all the evil, disgusting things we do so that we may be friends with God. Because of Jesus, we are forgiven. Because of Jesus, we have available to us guilt-free living. How do we obtain this? By believing in Jesus Christ and surrendering our life to Him. Just trust Him. Honestly ask Him to forgive you of your sins and He will. "God loved the world so much that he gave his one and only Son so that whoever believes in him may not be lost, but have eternal life. God did not send his Son into the world to judge the world guilty, but to save the world through him" (John 3:16-17 NCV).

POWER NUGGET #50:

JESUS CHRIST — The Great Motivator!

Paul Thigpen tells a cute story about his wife reading to their two year old son, Elijah, at bedtime. She was reading to him Jesus's story of the Good Samaritan. She got to the place in the story where the expert in the law confronted Jesus with a question. The lawyer asked Jesus, "And who is my neighbor?"

At that point little Elijah spoke up with what he thought was the answer, "I know! Mr. Rogers!"

I grew up on *Mr. Rogers' Neighborhood* and many of you probably did too. The values and lessons we learned through this program helped shape us to who we are today. Jesus Christ motivates us sometimes through programs such as Mr. Rogers's show. But the underlining motivation that Jesus uses to inspire us is LOVE. Jesus always motivates through love.

Let's take another look at the Good Samaritan story. For some of you this will be a visit to one of your favorite stories. For others of you it may be a first visit. Jesus tells this story in the book of Luke. The story goes as follows. There was a man who was walking on the road from Jerusalem to Jericho. This is a very dangerous road and robbers jumped the man. They didn't just take his money, they unmercifully beat him up. His body was bruised and bloody. His clothes were ripped. The robbers left the man lying on the edge of the road.

Some time had gone by when a Jewish priest came walking on the road. He saw the beaten man but decided to walk on the other side of the road and leave him there. Next, a Levite came by and he went up and looked at the injured man. After staring at the man, he decided he didn't want to bother with him either so he also walked by on the other side of the road. A little time later, a Samaritan came walking down the road. Now, you need to understand that the Jews hated the Samaritans. Samaritans were only part Jewish and so the Jews did not accept them. So what this Samaritan was about to do was very uncharacteristic. He saw the bloodied man. His heart went out to him. You see, it didn't matter if the man was of a different race or religion. It didn't matter whether they had anything in common or not. All that mattered was that he helped this man. The Samaritan was motivated by love. The Samaritan poured olive oil and wine on the man's wounds and then took him to an inn where he nursed him back to health.

The next morning, the Samaritan gave some money to the inn keeper and said: "Take care of this man. If this is not enough money then I will pay you back when I come again."

Jesus motivates us through love. We are to love our neighbors as ourself. Let's commit to living our lives like the Good Samaritan. That's what living is all about!

POWER NUGGET #51:

MAKE IT A GREAT DAY ... WITH GOD!

When we wake up every morning it is a blessing to be alive. The Bible says it this way, "This is the day that the Lord has made. Let us rejoice and be glad today!" (Psalm 118:24 NCV).

I want you to do something for me. Tomorrow morning when you get out of bed I want you to go to a window and repeat this scripture three times. Look outside at God's beauty when you do this. It doesn't matter if it is raining, snowing, or sleeting outside. It doesn't matter if you live in the country or in the city. Whatever the weather and wherever you are, it is going to be a great day because God made it and God made you. MAKE IT A GREAT DAY BECAUSE ... GOD LOVES YOU!

POWER NUGGET #52:

Sometimes the best thing to do is the hardest thing to do — "Wait on the Lord."

We live in a fast food age where we want everything as quickly as possible. We say things like, "I don't want to go there they take too long," or "Can you believe it took them the entire day to fix my car?" We don't want to wait. We want it now.

I am not exempt from this attitude. Patience has been a challenge for me. But one thing I have learned is that God's timing is perfect. If we wait on Him then He will send us what we need and when we need it. Dr. Robert Schuller said, "God's delays are not God's denials."

But why do we need to wait? Sometimes we aren't ready to receive the blessing. God has to get us ready first. Maybe we need to learn something first or maybe grow in our spiritual life. God knows and He has good planned for us (see Jeremiah 29:11). We all need to keep the faith, hold onto the dream, persevere, and "wait on the Lord." As it says in the Bible, "But the people who trust the Lord will become strong again. They will rise up as an eagle in the sky; they will run and not need rest; they will walk and not become tired" (Isaiah 40:31 NCV).

POWER NUGGET #53:

When you ask God a question He will sometimes ask you questions which will lead to the answer you are pursuing.

One day a father and his young son were taking a walk. Being a curious young boy, the son asked his dad, "What is electricity, Daddy?"

"Well, I really don't know. All I know is it makes things work like our television set," answered the father.

The two had walked a little ways further down the road when the boy looked up at his father and asked, "Daddy, how does gasoline make a car work?"

"Well, I really don't know that much about cars."

As they continued their walk the boy asked many more questions always with the same result. Finally the boy asked, "Daddy, does it bother you when I ask so many questions?"

The father looked lovingly down at his son and said, "Not at all. How else are you going to learn anything."

God feels the same way about his children (you and me). How else are we going to learn anything unless we ask Him. The difference between God and the dad in this little story is that God knows ALL the answers.

How does God answer our questions? This is called two-way prayer. After we ask our question we simply wait and listen to Him. Sometimes the answer will come in the form of a clear thought in our mind. Sometimes God will send the answer through another person. Sometimes God will even ask a question to answer our question. He might ask us what His Son Jesus would do in that situation. He might ask us what His word says. You see, God will never tell us to do something that goes against His own character. The Bible is His character. If it goes against the Bible, then God is against it. God will answer our questions in a variety of ways. Sometimes the answer comes quickly; sometimes it takes longer. So, my friend, keep asking God those questions ... and listen and wait for His answer.

POWER NUGGET #54:

Obeying the Golden Rule is the sign of a positive high self-esteem: "Do unto others as you would like them to do unto you." (The Bible)

The Golden Rule is all about love. Love for ourself and love for other people. But how can we truly follow the Golden Rule if we don't love ourself? Well, the truth is that it would be extremely difficult. If people would treat themselves like dirt then what would keep them from treating other people the same way? If they don't respect themselves then how can they show respect to other people?

I believe self-esteem and obedience is a key to living the Golden Rule. Self-esteem because we all need to learn to love and believe in ourselves. Obedience because we all need to obey Jesus' commands on how to love people including ourselves. Jesus said, "Love your enemies." He also said, "Love your neighbor as yourself." Unfortunately, many people are an enemy with themself. So, people in this situation need to be obedient to God by forcing themselves to love themselves. Simply be nice to yourself. Most of us know how to be nice to strangers. We need to treat ourselves the same way. In time, you will begin to love yourself and "your neighbor as yourself."

We can learn from a cute story about a six-year-old and her four-year-old brother. One day, these two children got into an argument. Before long, the two children began hitting each other.

The mother ran into the room and yelled, "Children, you stop that this instant! Be nice to each other! Haven't you ever heard of the Golden Rule?"

The six-year-old looked at her mother and exclaimed, "Yes, Mom, but he did it unto me first."

Yes, we are to do unto others but where this child made her mistake was that she didn't understand what we are to do unto others. What we are to do is love. The Golden Rule is love. Love for God, ourself, and other people. If we simply love, then we are fulfilling the Golden Rule.

POWER NUGGET #55:

Success is never created through doubt; success is always created through belief.

When I was a boy, my family had a great dog. We had gotten him when he was a puppy. He was a beagle and we named him Pongo (after the father dog in Disney's *101 Dalmatians*.) Yes, we named a beagle after a Dalmatian. When you're five years old lots of stuff makes sense.

When I was in high school, Pongo got cancer. This made me very sad. I loved my dog. We grew up together. He was always there for me. When I was upset and needed to talk, Pongo would sit there and just listen to me. Even though he didn't understand my words I believe he understood my emotions. Well, I didn't want to see my friend die so I prayed to God to heal my dog.

Some time went by and we took Pongo back to the vet. The vet was shocked. The cancer was completely gone. Pongo was healed. My friend, my question to you is if God would heal a boy's dog because of faith then what will God do for you because of your faith? You see, God loves us much more than animals. We are of utmost specialness to Him. He will bless us; He will heal us; He will prosper us only if we believe. "Look at the birds in the air. They don't plant or harvest or store food in barns, but your heavenly Father feeds them. And you know that you are worth much more than the birds ... God clothes the grass in the field, which is alive today but tomorrow is thrown into the fire. So you can be even more sure that God will clothe you. Don't have so little faith! Don't worry and say, 'What will we eat?' or 'What will we drink?' or 'What will we wear?' The people who don't know God keep trying to get these things, and your Father in heaven knows you need them. The thing you should want most is God's kingdom and doing what God wants. Then all these other things you need will be given to you" (Matthew 6: 26, 30-33 NCV).

POWER NUGGET #56:

It is better to err on the side of trust then to err on the side of judgmentalness.

Some people would say I trust too much. But I believe it is better to trust and get burned once in a while then to be judgmental and get burned all the time. Now you might be asking, "How can you get burned all the time if you don't trust people? Wouldn't you be protecting yourself?" Well, my friend, that is where the illusion is. When we don't trust anyone then we build up inside of ourselves paranoia, negative criticism towards others, and maybe even resentment. This creates a bomb in our belly ready to explode. The bomb must be defused.

"Does this mean we need to trust everyone all the time?" Unfortunately, not all people are trustworthy. Because of this fact, we need discernment on the character of people. Ask God and He will give you the discernment you need. And if you are carrying a bomb inside of you, God can help you defuse it if you let Him.

POWER NUGGET #57:

There is no success without Jesus Christ.

Once upon a time there lived a young man. This young man was very religious. He followed the scriptures and rules of the church legalistically. The young man was looked upon as having a great future in the church.

Yes, the young man was present when Stephen was stoned to death. And the young man supported this killing. You see, Stephen had been part of a group of troublemakers known as "the people of the Way." The young man despised these "people of the Way." They were teaching people a wrong path (so the young man thought). The young man was so zealous in his hatred for these people that he was allowed to go on a mission to Damascus to find and arrest these "people of the Way." He was then going to bring them back to Jerusalem where they hopefully would be executed.

The young man began his journey down the road to Damascus. All of a sudden there was a blinding light on the road. The light was so bright that it knocked the young man to the ground. As he was trying to see through the Light of Heaven, he heard a voice speaking to him, "Saul, Saul! Why are you persecuting me?"

Frightened and blinded, young Saul answered, "Wh, wh, who are you Lord?"

"I am Jesus. The One you are persecuting," said the Voice.

At that very moment Saul's life changed forever. He began to believe that these "people of the Way" also known as Christians were speaking the truth. That this Jesus was somehow the Son of God, the Messiah, the Christ. Saul gave his life to Jesus Christ and was saved of his sins. Through the changing of the condition of his heart, young Saul was transformed into the Apostle Paul and became the greatest evangelist for Jesus Christ ever to live.

You, too, can be successful in Christ Jesus. Just trust in Him and follow His leading in your life.

POWER NUGGET #58:

You can't count your chickens before they hatch but you can at least keep the eggs warm.

There is a story of two experienced fishermen who decided to go ice fishing. They walked onto the ice and cut two holes in the ice about 25 feet apart. They then each sat at their own hole and dropped in their lines. Nothing happened. Not even a nibble. This lack of success went on for hours.

Around mid-afternoon a young boy arrived. He confidently walked onto the ice and cut himself a hole between the two experienced fishermen. The boy had barely dropped his line in the water when he pulled up a fish. Then he pulled up another one ... and another ... and another. The two men were very confused about all of this. Finally, one of the men walked up to the boy and asked, "Young man, we have been here for hours and haven't even had a nibble. You show up and have success after success. What's your secret son?"

The boy looked up at the man and said, "Mmmm hmmm yhmm!"

"I didn't quite make that out son, what did you say?"

The boy repeated, "Mmmm hmmm yhmm!"

With a puzzled look on his face the man said, "I am sorry I can't understand you. Will you please speak a little more clearly?"

The boy spat a large amount of a brown substance into the palm of his hand and then looked up at the man and said, "You gotta keep your worms warm!"

Just as with eggs and worms, we need to keep our success warm. Think about salespeople. They have to service their customers continually if they want to keep them. Many times, they had to continually knock at the same door before that potential customer became a client. What I am trying to say is that we can't count our success before it happens but we can plan for it, expect it, work for it, and serve for it. The name of the game is servanthood. If you will serve people then you are successful! I think it was Dr. Robert Schuller who said, "Find a need and fill it." There are plenty of needs out there. Find them, fill them, and your needs will be filled too. As Jesus said, "Give and it shall be given to you" (The Bible).

POWER NUGGET #59:

There is no success without risk.

Risk is uncomfortable. Risk is scary. Risk is sometimes painful. But risk is necessary for success. If the Wright brothers weren't willing to risk death and take that first flight then we wouldn't have airplanes today. If Bill Gates wasn't willing to risk ridicule with a unique idea then Microsoft and computers would not be what they are today. If an individual was never willing to ask someone of the opposite sex out then we would have very few married people today.

Aesop has a tremendous fable which illustrates the importance of risk. The fable goes as follows:

An old cat was in the habit of catching all the mice in the barn.

One day the mice met to talk about the great harm that she was doing them. Each one told of some plan by which to keep out of her way.

"Do as I say, " said an old gray mouse that was thought to be very wise. "Do as I say. Hang a bell to the cat's neck. Then, when we hear it ring, we shall know that she is coming, and can scamper out of her way."

"Good! good!" said all the other mice, and one ran to get the bell.

"Now, which of you will hang this bell on the cat's neck?" said the old gray mouse.

"Not I! Not I!" said all the mice together. And they scampered away to their holes.

You see, risk is necessary for success. Choose success and ... choose risk.

POWER NUGGET #60:

The strength of human beings lies in their integrity.

There is the story of a man who was traveling through apple country. The man stopped beside the road to watch a farmer who was spraying his trees to keep the codling moths from damaging his apples. After some time, the man enquired of the farmer, "Why do you dislike the codling moth? What do you have against them?"

The farmer looked at the stranger and said, "It's not so much that I am against the codling moth. It's just that I am for my apples."

When people take a stand for something then by default everybody knows what they are against. A person of integrity stands up for certain values. Those are the values of truthfulness, trustworthiness, and honor. These values become the backbone of their life. The pillar that strengthens the roof under the bombardment of the enemy. And believe me, the enemy will attack when you stand up for integrity. But stand your ground and you will not be defeated. Sometimes the enemy will win the outward worldly battle but you must be certain you never lose the inward battle. With Jesus Christ on your side you can be sure. "So what should we say about this? If God is with us, no one can defeat us" (Romans 8:31 NCV).

POWER NUGGET #61:

Insecurity is an emotion which can only be conquered through faith.

Insecurity can be a paralyzing emotion that can keep us from reaching our dreams. Henry Ford had a successful way of conquering insecurity, worry, and anxiety. When asked if he ever worried, Mr. Ford replied, "No, I believe God is managing affairs and that He doesn't need any advice from me. With God in charge, I believe that everything will work out for the best in the end. So what is there to worry about?"

Mr. Ford was right. God is in charge. With God as the captain of our ship we can rest in confidence in Him. He has good planned for us and He will always take care of us. So, go out there and live life boldly with God.

POWER NUGGET #62:

When excitement is created, creativity will always follow.

Chip McGregor tells a true story about Larry Walters. Larry was a man who had a big dream. Larry's dream was to fly. He wanted to soar like an eagle with the ground zooming below him. In an attempt to fulfill his dream, Larry joined the Air Force after graduating from high school. But he was washed out of pilot candidacy because of poor eyesight. His dream appeared to be crushed.

After leaving the service, Larry had to live his dream through others. He would sit in his lawn chair in his backyard and watch the jets soar above him. Oh, how he wanted to fly.

Then one day while dreaming about flying, Larry got an idea. He excitedly went down to the local Army-Navy surplus store and bought a tank of helium and 45 heavy-duty weather balloons.

Larry strapped the balloons to his lawn chair and inflated them with the helium. He had anchored the chair to the bumper of his car as so it would not float away.

Larry packed some food and grabbed his BB gun. His idea was to float around for a while and then pop a balloon or two using the BB gun to bring himself softly and slowly back to earth.

He was ready to fulfill his dream. Seated in his captain's "lawn" chair he cut the chord anchoring him to the car. Instead of floating up slowly, the chair and Larry shot up like the space shuttle jumping off the launch pad. One hundred, two hundred, five hundred feet he rose into the air. But the chair didn't stop there. Up, up, up he went until he leveled off at eleven thousand feet.

Larry didn't know what to do. He feared popping the balloons with the BB gun because he thought it might unstable the chair and toss him out tumbling to earth. This was a thought he hadn't worried about when he was anchored safely and securely to his car bumper.

Things then got worse, much worse. The wind carried Larry and his homemade flying machine over towards Los Angeles International Airport. A Pan Am pilot radioed the tower explaining that they had just passed a guy in a lawn chair with a gun in his lap. Can you imagine the airline passengers' faces as they saw Larry out their window. They must have thought they were in an episode of *The Twilight Zone*.

As it began to get dark outside, the wind shifted and carried Larry out to sea. Finally a Navy helicopter came and rescued Larry. At last, Larry planted two feet on solid ground again where he was promptly arrested and hauled off to jail.

So, you might be saying, "Where's the lesson here?" The lesson is enthusiasm. When enthusiasm is created, the creative juices will begin to flow within our brains. This is when the breakthroughs will happen, breakthroughs which can lead us to our dreams. As bizarre as this story is, we have to admit that Larry lived his dream. He flew with the birds (as well as airline jets).

POWER NUGGET #63:

To be successful, one must find the balance between patience and assertiveness.

Success is found between the fine line of patience and assertiveness. I call this fine line positive harassment. In the beginning of my speaking career, I was trying to find a speakers' bureau who would book me for engagements. I finally found a guy who was interested but he wasn't moving quite as fast as I wanted him too. This is when I came up with the concept of positive harassment. I didn't call him every day because I didn't want to bug him. I didn't get cranky with him because I wasn't getting the bookings I wanted. Those things could be defined as harassment. What I did was call him just enough so he knew I was around. I kept myself in front of him so I would be on his mind. You see, he needed to want to book me for himself. I wanted to stay in eyeshot of him so he could see what he was missing

He liked what he saw and eventually hired me to work in his office. My job was to book myself as well as other speakers for engagements. What I learned was invaluable. I eventually went out on my own to book primarily myself and not as many other speakers. I decided it was more important for me to spend my time building my speaking career. It has been a great decision. But I am grateful to this man for giving me the opportunity to learn under his mentorship. He helped launch my career in a positive way. So learn the balance between patience and assertiveness and the rocket of your success will lift off the launchpad to newer and greater heights.

POWER NUGGET #64:

You will never reach greatness until you are willing to step out of the house.

Many of us have great dreams of accomplishing tremendous tasks but we never act on those dreams. We're afraid we might fail so we'd rather do nothing. I would rather strive for the mountain top and fail then to succeed at being comfortable and never leave my house. Step out of your comfortable surroundings and TAKE ACTION FOR YOUR DREAMS!

POWER NUGGET #65:

The belief we hold inside is a reflection of the life we'll live outside.

I remember a practice tennis match I played one time. The score was three all in the first set and then the next thing my practice partner knew was that I had won the first set six games to three. My practice partner said, "What happened?"

I said, "I told myself to raise my game."

"What do you mean, you told yourself to raise your game?" asked my partner.

What I was verbalizing very poorly was a positive self-expectation. This guy had never beaten me and I didn't expect him to now. I knew I was going to win so I just raised the level of my game to meet that expectation.

This particular partner tends to have a negative attitude. He thought the worst. He expected to lose and he did. I expected to win and I did. The belief we hold inside is everything. You see, a negative self-expectation is just as powerful as a positive self-expectation just in the wrong direction. A wrong direction down the path of failure and destruction.

A man who chose that negative path was Elvis Presley. "Come on, Mark! The king of rock and roll?" Yes, the king of rock and roll. Let me explain.

Elvis Presley's mother died of a heart condition at the age of 43. Elvis was so terrified that he would die of the same heart condition that he actually helped bring that condition upon himself.

Through worry and anxiety, Elvis' health started to deteriorate. His heart got weaker. His attitude got weaker. His negative self-expectation got stronger.

Elvis Presley was confident he would die by the time he reached the same age as his mother's death. He believed it with every ounce of his being. You know what happened? Elvis received what he believed. Elvis Presley died at age 43 and very near to the some month that his mother died. Coincidence? I don't think so!

Our attitude is important. Our belief system is powerful. What we believe has a way of coming true. Success coach Anthony Robbins tells a great story in his fabulous book, *Awaken the Giant Within*, of a man who believed in a positive self-expectation. A champion with a strong belief system who reached extraordinary success. That champion's name was Honda.

Even though he was still in school, Mr. Honda in the year 1938 took all the money he had and invested it in a small machine shop. It was his dream to develop his piston ring concept which he wanted to sell to Toyota Corporation.

After many hard hours of pain and sweat Honda finally presented his work to Toyota and they rejected it. They said his quality didn't meet their standards. Toyota then sent Honda back to school where he was cruelly teased by both his professors and his fellow students. They thought Honda's designs as well as Honda himself were crazy.

Many people would quit right there. Would you? How about Honda? NO WAY! Remember, champions expect to win! Honda continued to believe in himself and his work. Two more years went by before Toyota gave him the contract he desired.

At this time, the Japanese government was preparing for World War II and they refused to give Honda the concrete he needed to build his factory. But this challenge did not stop Honda. He was a champion. He rallied his team and they developed their own procedure for making concrete. They built their factory.

During the war, Honda's factory was bombed twice by American fighters. Did he quit now? It would certainly be understandable if he had. But that was not Honda. He pushed forward persistently. Honda turned this into a positive by gathering up the empty fuel tanks the fighters had dropped during their raids. Honda called the tanks "gifts from President Truman" because they provided him and his team with valuable raw materials which were not available in Japan.

Now, after all this an earthquake destroyed his factory and he was forced to sell his materials to Toyota. Most people would have given up by now. How about you? What else could Honda do but quit? Honda would not accept defeat. He knew that somehow, somewhere, there was a victory.

After the war, Japan went through a tremendous gasoline crunch. People were not allowed to use very much gasoline so out of desperation Honda strapped a small motor to his bicycle and made a motorized bike. Honda's neighbors loved this idea and asked if he would build some for them. Honda decided to so and eventually he ran out of motors.

Honda then got an idea. He thought, "Hmmm, what if I built a factory and manufactured these bikes?" But he didn't have any extra money. So what could he do? Forget about it? Not Honda. He wrote a personal letter to each of the eighteen thousand bicycle shop owners in Japan and he convinced five thousand of them to supply him with the capital he needed to fund his venture.

Honda built a factory and started manufacturing his motorized bikes. But the problem was these bikes were huge. They were big and bulky and only the most dedicated bicycle owners bought these bikes. So, Honda made a smaller, lighter version of his bike and it was an overnight success. He was even awarded the Emperor's Award for his achievements.

This success led to the automobiles we are so familiar with today. Because of one man's unstoppable positive self-expectation is why Honda Corporation is one of the finest companies in the world.

So, my friend, what do you believe? Can you succeed like Honda? You can if you believe you can. Hold on to your dreams and, like Honda, work them until they come true. YOU CAN DO IT!

POWER NUGGET #66:

Our emotions and our actions are tightly linked.

Anthony Robbins says that "Emotion is created by motion." Anthony is absolutely right. Have you ever heard of state management? Now, I am not talking about how to run a state such as Florida. I am talking about our states of mind and emotions.

Our states are affected by two things. One, our internal representations or how we look at the world. This is basically positive or negative thinking. Whether we look on the good side or the bad side does affect how we feel. Second, our states are affected by our physiology. Physiology can be defined as how we move our bodies. Movement of our bodies does create emotion.

Physiology is the quickest way to change how you feel. For example, let's say you have been watching television for two solid hours. You have not moved from your favorite chair. How do you feel? Probably a little lethargic. How can you get yourself to feel more energetic? By getting up and doing something. The movement will change your emotion.

We talked earlier about the "As if" principle. We simply act the way we want to be and the emotion will follow. If you want to have more energy, act the way you would if you had more energy. This will create the emotion of energy. If you want to be a person of courage then act as if you had courage. The emotion will follow. Physiology and positive thinking are powerful. Isn't the way God made us wonderful! God thought of all the details. He even packed POWER in a smile. Did you know that when we smile it releases a chemical in our brains that makes us feel good? Isn't that great? So, keep smiling and moving and create the emotions that you desire.

POWER NUGGET #67:

Plant a seed today ... expect a harvest tomorrow!

When a farmer plants a seed in the spring, he expects to harvest a crop in the fall. The same thing is true in our lives. When we plant a seed into a ministry or into someone's life then we can expect God to give us a harvest in our future. The Bible tells us "give and it shall be given unto you." This is a law that God has set forth. We can't out-give God. He is so generous. God has good planned for us (Jeremiah 29:11). So, we need to plant our time, finances, and our love. When we do this we not only help other people, we are also helping ourselves. WOW! Its a win-win way of life.

POWER NUGGET #68:

People are tremendous assets when you look for the best in them and commit yourself to helping them bring out that best.

William Bennett has a tremendous poem in his book *The Book of Virtues*. The poem is about helping people. It is a poem about meeting people where they are and helping them where they need it most — by being a friend. The poem is titled "The House by the Side of the Road" and it is by Sam Walter Foss (1858-1911):

There are hermit souls that live withdrawn
*   In the peace of their self-content;*
There are souls, like stars, that swell apart,
*   In a followless firmament;*
There are pioneer souls that blaze their paths
*   Where highways never ran;*
But let me live by the side of the road
*   And be a friend to man.*

Let me live in a house by the side of the road,
*   Where the race of men go by —*
The men who are good and the men who are bad,
*   As good and as bad as I.*
I would not sit in the scorner's seat,
*   Or hurl the cynic's ban;*

Let me live in a house by the side of the road
  And be a friend to man.

I see from my house by the side of the road,
  By the side of the highway of life,
The men who press with the ardor of hope,
  The men who are faint with the strife.
But I turn not away from their smiles nor their tears —
  Both parts of an infinite plan;
Let me live in my house by the side of the road
  And be a friend to man.

Let me live in my house by the side of the road
  Where the race of men go by —
They are good, they are bad, they are weak,
    they are strong.
  Wise, foolish — so am I.
Then why should I sit in the scorner's seat
  Or hurl the cynic's ban? —
Let me live in my house by the side of the road
  And be a friend to man.

If every owner of every business in the world would adopt this attitude, can you imagine how much happier and successful the employees and the company would be? If all parents would raise their children with this attitude, can you imagine how the world's children would be happier with positive self-images? If everyone would adopt this attitude, can you see how much better the world would be?

POWER NUGGET #69:

The gift of joy will come to you when you give the gift of yourself to someone else.

One of the greatest joys in life is when we can help someone else's dreams come true. It might be something simple like reading a book to the blind or being a big brother or sister to a youth in trouble. Very often, time is the greatest gift we can give to another person. Fancy cars and big houses aren't all that important to a child. What's important is whether mom and dad have time to listen to them, or play ball with them, or go to school plays, or have dinner with them. This is what is important to a child. And you know what? There is a little child in you and in me.

Let me share with you the story of a family who truly learned the joys of giving. It is a story by Paula Palangi McDonald.

Ellen had taken about all she could handle. It had been a long winter day with the kids cooped up in the house. Her four little angels had been showing their bad side all day long. They argued; they fought; they drove their mother crazy, just like all normal children who have been cooped up too long. The worst were the two oldest, Eric and Kelly. Eric was the oldest, with Kelly only one year younger.

The Christmas season was fast upon them with Christmas only one month away. But the McNeal household had more of a Halloween mood than a festive Christmas feeling.

As the tension began to consume her, Ellen got an idea. Years earlier, she remembered her grandmother telling her about an old custom which helped people discover the true meaning of Christmas.

She rounded up the kids and lined them — Eric, Kelly, Lisa, and the littlest Mike.

Ellen said to her children, "How would you kids like to start a new Christmas tradition this year?" She explained it was kind of like a game but only could be played by people who could keep a secret. All the kids screamed that they could keep a secret.

Ellen explained that this year they were going to surprise Baby Jesus with the softest bed in the world. They would fill a small crib with straw for Him to sleep in. Here is where the secret came in. The straw that is put into the crib would signify the good deeds each of them did for someone else. The secret was that you could not tell anyone who you were doing the good deeds for.

Eric a little confused asked, "But who will we do the good deeds for?"

"We'll do them for each other," explained his mother. "Once a week we will draw names to see who we will get to do good deeds for. When Daddy gets home tonight we will all draw names."

Ellen was looking forward to seeing her husband Mark's reaction to the changed mood of their children. It was beginning to feel more like Christmas all the time at the McNeil home.

That night all six of them drew names from Mark's winter hat. The children were filled with excitement. They chose their secret name one by one. Unable to read yet, Mark whispered little Mike's name in his ear. Mike then quickly ate the piece of paper to make sure the secret was safe. Eric then chose a piece of paper. He looked at it and immediately a frown came over his face when he saw the name. Ellen and Mark then selected and the family was ready to begin their new Christmas tradition.

Little by little the small crib began to fill with straw as the McNeils filled their lives with good deeds. One family member might find his bed made, or his shoes shined, or her nightgown laid out for the evening. The house was filled with Christmas cheer.

Week after week the McNeils chose names and continued to do good deeds for each other. The crib was nearly full. Now, it was time to choose names for the last time. It was the night before Christmas Eve. The family gathered around with anticipation for this last drawing of names. One by one they all drew names again. Finally, the hat came to Eric. There was only one name left. He picked up the piece of paper and looked at the name. A look of pain and anguish came over Eric's face. He turned and ran out of the room. Everyone immediately jumped up to follow but Ellen stopped them and said that she would go.

She found her little boy in his room putting on his coat. In his other hand was a cardboard suitcase. Eric said to his mother, "I have to leave. If I don't, I'll ruin Christmas."

"But why?" asked Ellen. "And where will you go?"

Eric said he could sleep in his snow fort for a couple of days and he promised he would come home right after Christmas.

Ellen started to say something to convince her little boy of staying when Mark came up and put his hand on her shoulder and shook his head to wait. After Eric slumped through the front door Mark said to his worried wife, "Give him a few minutes alone. I think he needs that. Then you can talk to him."

After a few minutes, Ellen walked across the street where Eric was sitting on a snowbank. It had begun to snow and Eric was beginning to be covered with the white blanket. "What's wrong, Eric? I know something has been bothering you. Please tell me what it is, honey."

"Don't you get it, Mom? Every week I got stuck with the same stupid name. Every week I got stuck with Kelly. I hate Kelly. I tried to do good deeds for her. I went in her room every night when nobody was watching and I fixed her bed. I even laid out her stupid nightgown. And when I let her use my race car she smashed it into the wall like she always does. Every week I thought it would be different but I always got Kelly. If I stay I will ruin Christmas. I just know I will end up beating up Kelly."

Ellen said to her hurting little boy, "Eric, I know it was hard for you to do all those good deeds for Kelly. And that it is why I am so proud of you. Every one of your good deeds should count double because they were so difficult for you. Maybe that is what Christmas is all about. Giving love when it is hard to love. Eric, you probably added the most important straws to Baby Jesus' bed this year.

Ellen offered to switch names with Eric so he could earn some easy straws. Eric finally agreed with his mother and they went back into the house.

Throughout the next day, the little crib was filled to overflowing with straw. As bedtime approached, Ellen snuck up to turn down Kelly's bed and lay out her nightgown. As she walked into the room, a surprise of joy filled Ellen's heart. Someone had already fixed Kelly's bed and laid out her nightgown. And on the bed next to the pillow sat a beautiful little toy race car.

That's what life is all about. Let's commit our lives to giving where it really matters ... people.

POWER NUGGET #70:

A positive thinker is a person who always looks for the best in him/herself, all people, and in all situations. Thus, the positive thinker brings out the best in him/herself, all people, and in all situations.

The law of attraction says, "Like attracts like." If we look for the best then we'll find the best and bring that into our lives. But by the same law of attraction if we look for the worst then we'll find that and bring it into our lives. You see, it was Dr. Norman Vincent Peale, the modern father of positive thinking, who said, "Any fact facing us is not as important as our attitude toward it, for that determines our success or failure."

So, there are two choices we have for the direction of our lives. We can choose the positive path or we can choose the negative path. The choice is ours. Let me share with you the story of two little boys who chose opposite paths. One of the boys was a negative thinker while the other was a positive thinker. On one particular Christmas, their father decided to perform an experiment with his sons. The custom in this family was that one boy would find his present on one side of the Christmas tree and the other boy would find his on the other side.

The negative thinking boy found his present and it was a brand new, shiny bike. The boy said, "I don't want it. It is too dangerous. I just know I will crash and hurt myself."

Meanwhile, his positive thinking brother found his present which was a simple box of manure. A smile came over the boy's face. He looked at his parents and said excitedly, "Mom, Dad, you are so good to me. This is the best present ever — A PONY!" Be a positive thinker and look for the best.

POWER NUGGET #71:

Champions are people who are willing to risk failure in order to succeed.

As we discussed before, risk is necessary for success. But there is good risk and there is bad risk. Good risk is when you put yourself on the line for a greater good. Good risk is an exercise in discernment. Seeking God's wisdom is a key to good risk. Bad risk is foolish recklessness. It is jumping forward without seeking God's wisdom. Bad risk is selfishly thinking only about your needs. Bad risk is something to avoid at all costs. Yes, good risk is necessary for success but before you jump, talk it over with God.

POWER NUGGETS #72:

Failure is not a bad thing; it is a stepping stone to success.

When you are teaching a baby how to be toilet trained, how many messes do you allow the child to make before you stop him and not allow him to try again? You may be saying, "What, are you kidding? My child is going to continue to try until he succeeds. Otherwise there would be millions of adults running around with diapers in their pants." You are absolutely right. So, why is it different for us when we are striving to reach our dreams? It is no different. We just give up too soon. If we learn from our failures, then they put us one step closer to living our dreams ... if we don't quit. Calvin Coolidge said, "Nothing in the world can take the place of persistence. Talent will not; nothing is more common than the unsuccessful man with talent. Genius will not; unrewarded genius is almost a proverb. Education will not; the world is full of educated derelicts. Persistence and determination alone are omnipotent. The slogan 'press on' has solved and always will solve the problems of the human race."

The great inventor Thomas Edison understood that failure was just a stepping stone to success. It took Edison 50,000 experiments before he succeed with his new storage battery. One time Edison exclaimed to an assistant, "Results! Results? Why, man, I have gotten a lot of results. I know 50,000 things that won't work."

Follow the lead of Thomas Edison. Have the courage to fail today so you can succeed tomorrow!

160

POWER NUGGET #73:

Failure is a sign of great courage.

It took Thomas Edison something like 10,000 attempts before he succeeded at inventing the electric light bulb. But he knew with each attempt he was getting closer to victory. It takes courage to keep going in the face of adversity. You have courage; you are a champion.

POWER NUGGET #74:

Success is constantly improving to be your best where you are and with what you have.

Evangelist Mike Murdock says, "Whatever you possess today is enough to create anything else you will ever want in your future." Life is a journey of growth. Don't be satisfied with the status quo. Seek improvement always. It doesn't matter how successful we may already be; we can be better. We can learn more. We can improve. That's the goal: improvement through growth.

Thomas Edison told the story of how he got fired twice. Mr. Edison explained: "I got fired twice. The first time was when I was a telegraph operator. It was my fault, all right, but I got so interested in the dinged machine and its workings that I began to see how I could improve it. But I forgot all about the messages that were coming over the wire, and I left a lot of messages unsent and undelivered. Of course, they discharged me, and I didn't blame them."

With a chuckle and a smile on his face Mr. Edison continued, "Then I got a job in an office, and there were a fearful lot of rats; terribly old office, you know. I got up a thing that killed them like flies — the same with cockroaches. The floor used to be covered with dead roaches, and they fired me for that!"

Life and success are about improvements. Improving ourselves and improving our surroundings. Where can you improve today? What new thing can you learn? What new action can you take today which will change your life for the better? The answer to these questions is a roadmap to your desired future.

POWER NUGGET #75:

Success is a four letter word spelled — GROW!

Aristotle said, "The difference between an educated and uneducated man is the same difference as between being alive and being dead." Life is a journey of growth. I don't believe one can be truly happy if one is not seeking growth and improvement. Without growth, there is stagnation. Refresh the water of your soul — GROW!

POWER NUGGETS #76:

Love is a tiny word with huge assets.

Love is the greatest power in the world. The Bible tells us that God is love. When we allow God to love through us then we are truly making a difference as His ambassadors to a hurting world. Dan Clark tells a great story which illustrates God's love to a hurting world. This story is found in the book *Chicken Soup for the Soul* written and compiled by Jack Canfield and Mark Victor Hansen. In the story, Dan tells about his friend Paul. One Christmas, Paul's brother gave him the present of a shiny, brand new car. It was Christmas Eve and Paul was looking forward to the drive home from work in his new car. As Paul made his way to the parking lot, he noticed a little street urchin walking around his car. The little boy noticed Paul and said, "Mister, is this your car?"

"Yes, it is," said Paul. "My brother gave it to me."

"You mean, you didn't have to pay nothin for it?" asked the boy.

"That's right," said Paul.

"Gee, I wish I ..." and the boy hesitated.

Well, Paul knew exactly what the little boy was going to say. Of course he was going to say, "I wish I had a brother like that." Well, that is not what the little boy said. When he finished his sentence it went like this, "Gee, I wish I could be a brother like that."

This was Paul's first surprise of the day. He was so touched by the little boy's expression of love that he offered to give him a ride in the shiny, new car.

They hadn't been driving too long when the boy asked Paul if he could drive him home to his neighborhood. Paul knew exactly what the boy wanted. He wanted all his neighbors to see him come home in a shiny, new car. This is when Paul got his second surprise of the day.

As soon as Paul stopped the car in front of the little boy's house, the street urchin jumped out and ran up two steps and into the house. He was gone for a little while and then came back. Cradled in his arms was his crippled little brother. The urchin gently sat his brother on the steps and said, "See there, Buddy. There it is. Just like I told you upstairs. And someday, Buddy, I am going to buy you one just like it and then we can go see all those Christmas windows I've been telling you about."

Paul was so struck with emotion that he got out of the car and walked over to Buddy and picked him up and sat him in the car. Paul, Buddy, and Buddy's big brother (I call him "The Dream Builder") went for a Christmas ride I am sure they will cherish for the rest of their lives. And that is the day Paul truly understood what Jesus meant when He said, "It is more blessed to give."

Wow, that is what love is all about. When we plant a seed of love in someone's dream, the gift of love will always flow back to us — many times in ways we don't expect. BE A "DREAM BUILDER" AND LIVE A LIFE OF LOVE!

POWER NUGGET #77:

Men and women: Perfectly suited ... Explosively different!

Have you ever wonderered how men and women ever get together? We are so different yet we are drawn to each other. Why? That is what God intended. We need to look at our differences as opportunities for greater intimacy. Men and women think and communicate differently. When we begin to understand these differences, then we can communicate more effectively with the opposite sex. We begin to appreciate our differences and we also begin to better understand ourselves. Yes, sometimes men and women are explosively different but more importantly we are PERFECTLY SUITED. As a wise person has pointed out, "Creation of woman from the rib of man: She was not made of his head to top him; nor out of his feet to be trampled upon by him; but out of his side to be equal with him, under his arm to be protected, and near his heart to be loved."

SECTION THREE
Going All The Way

Sometimes on the road of success, we begin to run out of gas. This section, "Going All The Way," will keep your gas tank full and your engine running strong.

POWER NUGGET #78:

Success is a journey that never rests.

"Does this mean I can never take a vacation? If that's true then won't I become a workaholic? If that is the only way to succeed then I don't want anything to do with it." These may have been some of the questions that came to your mind after reading this Power Nugget. Believe me, I am not trying to create a society of workaholics. After all, I like vacations too. I need rest and relaxation just like you. R&R actually helps us succeed even more. It recharges our batteries and puts us a step ahead of the competition who works all the time nonstop. Well, you might be saying, "Okay, Mark, then what on earth do you mean by 'Success is a journey that never rests'?" I am talking about our attitudes. Our attitudes are with us every day of our lives. At work, our attitudes are with us. At home, our attitudes are with us. At play, our attitudes are with us. This is why we can never take a rest when it comes to our attitudes. We always have to be conscious of what we are focusing on and what we allow to come into our minds. Our attitudes create or destroy our present and future success. But don't worry if you do not like the attitude you have today because you can change your attitude.

Let me share with you a quote from preacher and author Charles Swindoll. I hope it is as helpful for you as it has been for me. "The longer I live, the more I realize the impact of attitude on life.

Attitude, to me, is more important than facts. It is more important than the past, than education, than money, than circumstances, than failures, than successes, than what other people think or say or do. It is more important then appearance, giftedness, or skill. It will make or break a company ... a church ... a team ... a home. The remarkable thing is we have a choice every day regarding the attitude we will embrace for that day. We cannot change our past ... we cannot change the fact that people will act in a certain way. We cannot change the inevitable. The only thing we can do is play on the one string we have, and that is our attitude ... I am convinced that life is 10 percent what happens to me and 90 percent how I react to it. And so it is with you ... we are in charge of our Attitudes."

POWER NUGGET #79:

Man's approval means nothing unless you already have God's approval which means eternal life.

Many times the temptation in life is to please people at the expense of pleasing God. George Washington said, "If, to please the people, we offer what we ourselves disapprove, how can we afterward defend our work? Let us raise a standard to which the wise and honest can repair." We need to raise the standard by lifting our eyes to Jesus. By asking the question, "What would Jesus want me to do?" or "What would Jesus do in this situation?" By so doing, we will more closely live the life God wants us to live. By pleasing God, we won't always please our fellow man. But what is more important: pleasing the Creator of the universe who holds your life in His hands or some imperfect human being walking on God's earth?

POWER NUGGET #80:

Winning a game by cheating is not victory but losing in life.

Unfortunately, many people do not understand this concept. Their philosophy is "anything goes as long as I win" or "the end result supports the means." But that philosophy could not be further from the truth. Jesus said that those who try to save their own life would lose their life and those who gave up their life for His sake would find their life.

I am thinking of a story which seems to be appropriate. An American diplomat was sent to Greece after World War II on one of his first assignments. At that time, Greece was in the middle of civil war. Also, the British considered Greece to be within their influential leadership. The American diplomat was sent on this special two-man mission to investigate the Greek crisis.

On the first night they had free, the American diplomat and his junior partner stopped by the only club under Greek influence in Athens. At the bar there were two or three gruff Englishmen who were telling anti-American jokes in rather loud voices. The junior American leaned over to his senior partner and whispered, "Let's leave. We don't have to listen to this garbage."

The American diplomat said to his young apprentice, "No! That is exactly what they want us to do. Tell you what, I will tell a story instead." The American diplomat said to the Englishmen in a loud voice, "Have you heard the story about the Swiss plane on its way to Lisbon during the war whose engines began to croak in mid-air?"

The Engishmen acted disinterested but a Greek at the bar spoke up with an enthusiastic, "No!"

The American diplomat began to tell his story, "Well, since it was a neutral plane it carried people from different countries. After the trouble began, the pilot announced that they would have to dump some weight because they were losing altitude. The pilot said that one of the passengers would have to jump if the rest were to be saved. Unfortunately, there were no parachutes on board. The passengers consisted of a German, an Italian, a Greek, and a Britisher. They all looked at each other and decided to draw straws.

"The German drew the short straw and went to the door for his plunge into the great beyond. He saluted and said, 'Heil Hitler,' and jumped out of the plane.

"Some time had gone by when the pilot announced again that they were losing altitude and somebody else would have to jump. The passengers drew straws again. This time, the Italian drew the short straw. He went to the door and saluted. He then said, 'Viva Il Duce,' as the rest of the passengers prepared to push him out of the plane.

"After awhile, the pilot announced again that someone would have to go. The remaining two passengers drew straws. The Englishman lost. He rose to his feet and walked to the door. He said proudly, 'THERE WILL ALWAYS BE AN ENGLAND,' and then he pushed the Greek out."

Who won in this humorous story? The Englishman? The pilots? Who? I say it is the ones who sacrificed themselves for the others. Winning is giving of yourself. It might be sharing the last piece of pie with a friend. It might be running an errand for your neighbor when you would rather be going to the movies. It might be sacrificing your life to save another. This is winning! This is life!

POWER NUGGET #81:

All people deserve respect as children of God.

How does it make you feel when people do not listen to your ideas? How does it make you feel when someone cuts in line in front of you? How does it make you feel when people insult you? Not too good, right? All people deserve respect just for being born. I dare say that both you and I have committed all three of these offenses toward others. We know how they felt when we did so. You and I need to commit right now to showing respect to everyone who crosses our path. As the Good Book says, "Do unto others as you would want them to do unto you."

POWER NUGGET #82:

Is a champion someone who has never fallen? NO! The champion just keeps getting back up.

Champions are very often the people who have fallen the most. They just refuse to quit. Persistence is a way of life for them. Let me tell you the story of a friend of mine. His name is Omar Periu. When Omar was seven years old he found himself in Miami International Airport with his mother and brother. They had just left their home in Cuba for what Omar knew was the last time.

Communism was spreading around the world and it was stealing the freedom from the Cuban people. Omar's father knew it was time to get his family out of Cuba. Because Castro's regime was watching him so closely, Omar's father felt it necessary to send his family to America ahead of him. He met his family a few weeks later.

This was a tough time for the Periu family. They had no money and no extended family to help them. A few months later during the winter of 1961, they went to Joliet, Illinois, with the help of a church.

Omar's dad was an educated man with a passion for success for himself and more importantly his family. He was able to get a job as a mechanic and they found a small apartment in which to live.

School was tough for Omar and his brother Ed. They couldn't speak English and it was common for the other kids to make fun of them or even to steal their bikes. But Omar had learned a valuable lesson from his father. Many times he would hear these words from his father, "It doesn't matter who you are, where you're from or what color you are. You can do anything you put your mind to." These words inspired Omar to overcome his challenges in life. These words would be a key to his success later on.

The Perius are a talented family musically and Omar is no exception. As the years went by, Omar's passion for music blossomed. He worked in a stone quarry as a laborer and also received a scholarship to put himself through college. He studied opera and music at Southern Illinois University. After two years of college, Omar went back to work at the quarry to save up money so he could move to California.

Omar had a dream. He wanted to cut his own records. That is why he wanted to go to California. But as you are probably aware, the music business is not an easy one to break into. Omar had to take a job selling health club memberships. The job at least paid the bills.

Omar then met Tom Murphy who was one of the owners of the health club. Omar knew that if he wanted to be wealthy then he had to do the same things the wealthy did (another lesson from his father). So, Omar asked Mr. Murphy if they could talk.

Mr. Murphy just so happened to be the business partner of Tom Hopkins who is one of the nation's top sales trainers. Mr.

Murphy recommended that Omar begin attending sales training seminars, reading motivational self-help books, and listening to sales tapes. Mr. Murphy also introduced Omar to many successful business men and women and their success materials.

Well, it didn't take Omar long to become the top salesperson in the company. He eventually owned nine of his own health clubs. But Omar still had an empty feeling inside. He still had not reached his dream to cut his own record.

After many rejections from record companies, Omar took his father's advice and bought his own record company. Now he could cut his own records. Omar went on to be named "Best Latin Male Vocalist" and "Entertainer of the Year" in 1986, 1987, and 1988 "CHIN de PLATA" and "OTTO."

Today, Omar is a successful professional speaker with Tom Hopkins International. This is how I met Omar. Tom Hopkins speaks on many of Peter Lowe International's "SUCCESS" seminars. I did some work behind the scenes for Peter Lowe. It was an honor to work side by side with Omar. He is a great man of integrity, courage, persistence, loyalty, and self-sacrifice. He is a true champion. Let us follow Omar's lead by being champions who once in a while will fall down ... and always get back up!

POWER NUGGET #83:

Attack your enemies with LOVE!

How does it make you feel when someone does wrong towards you? How does it make you feel when someone lies to you? How does it make you feel when someone hurts someone close to you? Angry? Probably. How do you react? How do you want to react? Sometimes you just want to bop them in the head. Right? I know the feeling. But how are we supposed to react to these difficult people in our lives? Jesus said we are to love our enemies and do good to them. Why, that's not justice. Or is it? When we love our enemies it not only helps us but them as well. Many a war has been averted because one of the parties chose love instead of violence. Loving and forgiving our enemies is healthier for us spiritually, emotionally, and physically. When we choose to love our enemies it rids us of all those negative harmful emotions of hate and envy. Also, loving our enemies will either frustrate them because we are not giving them the reaction they want or it might actually began to help them change to an action of love as well. So, when someone does you wrong just — STOP, PAUSE, and choose to LOVE!

POWER NUGGET #84:

It takes more courage to be a man of peace than it does to be a man of war.

It is more difficult to walk away from a fight then it is to throw the first punch. Why is that? I think many times it is because of pride. We think people will look down on us or call us a whimp if we refuse to fight. It is true that some people will make fun of us. But their opinion is not important. Many people will respect us for our courage, self-control, and strength. These are the opinions we need to listen to.

Sometimes as much as we try to avoid it, the fight/war is inevitable. But does that mean there has to be violence? NO! Think about how Dr. Martin Luther King, Jr. fought his war. He fought it with words and ideas. One can kill the soldier but he can't kill the soldier's idea. Dr. King's messages of racial reconciliation ring just as strong today as they did the day they flowed from his mouth. Violence is the last choice of action, an action we hope never has to be taken. Violence is never desirable.

Compare this with the disturbed people who bomb abortion clinics. Is that a proper way to fight? NO! I hate abortion. It is murder and a sin before Almighty God but I would never bomb an abortion clinic. Two sins do not make a right. We need to battle the abortionists in the arena of ideals. How would Jesus battle abortionists? By hitting them? How about killing them? No,

Jesus would tell them the truth. He would tell them it is murder. He would tell them that God has special plans for the unborn even before they are formed in the womb. He would tell them that even though they are sinning that He always loves them. Jesus knew how to fight — with TRUTH and LOVE!

POWER NUGGET #85:

A challenge is simply an opportunity in disguise.

Some off the toughest times of my life were the times I grew the most. By no means do I want to go back and live those times again, but I would not trade who I am today because of those tough times. I am a better person today because I grew through those challenging times.

I have played a lot of tennis throughout the years. A few years ago, I suffered a major injury to my right shoulder during a doubles match. I tore the shoulder capsule and dislocated my shoulder out towards my back.

I underwent surgery and remember being told afterwards by my father that the surgery may not have been a success. There was more damage than originally anticipated. I spent the next three weeks with my shoulder virtually immobile. I then went through five months of physical therapy. The goal was to keep the shoulder stable and return me to as much range of motion as possible.

All during this time I held a dream inside. I wanted to play tennis again. I wanted to play in the GTE Indy Open which was a semi-pro tournament. I had never played in a semi-pro tournament before. But I believed I could do it. I believed I could overcome this injury and play better than I had ever played before.

After a few months of hard work, I got back on the court and finally in a tournament. Those first few tournaments were rough.

My shoulder could only handle so much stress and then I would have to start to serve underhanded to protect my shoulder. Do you know how hard it is to win a match serving underhanded? But I kept at it and my hard work and belief payed off.

Eight months after surgery I stepped onto a very special tennis court. It was a court hosting the GTE Indy Open. I was there! I made it! I got beat first round in singles but I was there. The dream was accomplished. The icing on the cake was teaming up with my good friend Arnel Gallanosa for the doubles competition. We got to the quarterfinals where we played the number one seeded team in the tournament. We got beat that day but what an experience it was. Not bad for a kid who was lying on an operating table just eight months earlier.

The lessons I learned of faith and persistence made all the pain I went through all worthwhile (not fun but worthwhile). When tough times come, hang tough and discover what you can learn ... that's the opportunity in disguise.

POWER NUGGET #86:

Attacking a person is judgmental; confronting a negative behavior is correction.

Once upon a time, there lived a great warrior and king by the name of Genghis Khan. He was such a great conqueror that his empire ranged from eastern Europe all the way to the Sea of Japan. One day when he was home, Genghis Khan decided to take a group out in the woods for a relaxing day of hunting. They had a great day even though the hunting was not as good as they had hoped.

When it was time to go home, Genghis Khan decided to take a longer path home riding all alone. He had had with him on the hunt his favorite pet hawk. In those days, hawks were used for hunting. Now as he silently rode along, Genghis was all alone. His hawk had left his side and flown away. Genghis was not worried. He knew the hawk would find its way home.

The longer he rode, the thirstier Genghis became. Finally, he spotted a trickle of water coming down over the edge of a rock. He grabbed his cup and jumped off his horse.

It took a long time to fill the cup because the trickle was so slow. Finally, the cup was filled almost to the rim. Genghis lifted the cup to his mouth and was just about to take a drink when a blur came out of nowhere and knocked the cup out of his hand. The water spilled all over the ground. What could have done this?

Genghis looked around and saw his pet hawk. Now, why in the world would his hawk do such a thing?

Genghis tried again. This time he did not wait so long. When the cup was half full he started to lift the cup again. The bird again sailed down and knocked the cup out of his hand. Genghis was now growing angry and impatient with his pet. He tried to drink a third time with the same result. He filled the cup again. Genghis then drew his sword. He was determined to get a drink even if he had to kill the hawk. This time as the bird knocked the cup from Genghis's hand, he swung his sword at the bird. The bird fell to the ground bleeding to death. However, the cup had fallen between two rocks where Genghis could not reach it.

Genghis was still determined to have a drink of water. He began to climb the hill to find the spring from which the trickle sprang. At last, he found the spring. But what was lying in it was a large dead poisonous snake. His pet (friend) had saved his life. If Genghis had drunk from this spring he would have surely died.

Genghis Khan learned a valuable lesson that day. Anger is an emotion that can blind us from the truth. We must follow Jesus Christ's example on how to handle anger. Christ became angry too from time to time but he never acted irrationally. He calmed His anger through time and wisdom and always acted appropriately. We must never attack anyone but simply confront (when necessary) with truth and love.

POWER NUGGET #87:

The beginning of humanity is spelled — LOVE!

Is it truly possible to be human without love? I don't think so. Man is the only creature that we know for sure is capable of feeling and expressing love. In fact, love is the underlying motivation of our entire lives. We desire to love and be loved. This is what humanity is all about. If this is true, then why is there so much pain and suffering in the world? Well, I believe that many times it is because we don't know how to express love in a wise and meaningful way. Many times in our desperate search for love, we end up hurting other people and ourselves in the process. This is a sad state of affairs. We must learn to love. We need to love other people the way they need to be loved, not the way we want to love them.

Have you ever wondered why it is called a sacrifice fly in baseball? It is because the batter sacrifices himself to move ahead the base runner. How about in war? It seems like almost every war movie has someone courageously giving his life to save his buddy's life. But did you know this really does happen in war? In fact, when you think about it, every veteran is this kind of hero. Even if a veteran never served during a war, he knew that war could break out at any time and he would have to put his life on the line. On the line for whom? The answer: YOU AND ME. This reminds me of another Person who sacrificed His life to save others.

187

He was nailed to a cross around two thousand years ago. He was willing to die so that you and I might live. His name is Jesus Christ. He is LOVE!

POWER NUGGET #88:

Accountability is a blessing. It helps keep us on God's road. It is wise to have a friend or two who loves you enough to tell you what you need to hear, not necessarily what you want to hear.

I am blessed to have three such friends in my life. They are my brothers in Jesus Christ. Their names are John, Curt, and Paul. The four of us meet regularly to study the Bible. We discover that many times through our study sessions we start discussing many tangents in our lives. It is through these tangents that God uses us to keep one another accountable to God's will for our lives. For example, one of us might mention a situation in our life which is challenging or frustrating to us. At this time, the other three are there to listen and offer support through love and biblical imput. I have found these experiences with these three great men of God very enlightening and rewarding. I encourage you to find such a small group for your life.

POWER NUGGET #89:

If you aren't connected with God, then you aren't connected with life.

Brian Harbour tells a wonderful story in his book *Rising Above the Crowd* of a little boy who was born many years ago in east Tennessee. The little boy is Ben Hooper. Ben was born to an unwed mother and was treated badly by the townsfolk. Parents didn't want "a boy like that" playing with their children. Many times people would whisper just in earshot of Ben and his mother, "Did you ever figure out who his daddy is?" Can you imagine the pain this must have caused Ben and his mother?

When Ben was twelve years old a new preacher came to town. Ben began hearing great things about this new preacher. Ben decided he had to find out for himself. So, one Sunday Ben snuck into the church after the service began. He didn't want to be noticed by the townspeople. Ben loved hearing the preacher speak. It made Ben feel good. He liked what he heard. There was hope after all. Ben then snuck out before the service was over so the people would not see him. Ben came back to the little church on Sunday again and again, always sneaking in and sneaking out.

Finally, on one Sunday, Ben got so caught up in the service he forgot to leave early. When the service was over Ben tried to leave as quickly as he could but he got caught in a traffic jam of people.

Ben felt a hand on his shoulder. It was the preacher. The preacher asked little Ben, "Whose boy are you?" A hush came over the stunned congregation. They had wanted to know the answer to that question for years. A small smile came over the preacher's face as he said, "Oh, I know whose boy you are. The family resemblance is unmistakable. You are a child of God!"

Ben did have a Father, a Heavenly Father. The young preacher patted Ben on the rear like a coach encouraging an athlete and sent him off with these words, "That's quite a heritage you've got there, boy! Now, go and see to it that you live up to it."

My friend, you are from a great blood line. You are in the family of God. You are intimately connected with God and thus with life.

POWER NUGGET #90:

Determination is the power that keeps a dream alive.

What could you accomplish if you had ten years to finish it? How about twenty years? Thirty years? The truth is if we continue persistently to push towards our dreams then we will live a more successful life.

Colonel Remy tells the story of an old fable that was spread during World War II after the fall of France. In July of 1940, England was battling the enemy alone. As the story goes, Hitler invited Churchill to a secret conference in Paris. When Churchill arrived he was escorted to the Chateau of Fontainebleau, where he found sitting at a table by the famous carp pool none other than Hitler and Mussolini.

Hitler lost no time and got right to the point. "All right, Churchill! This is the situation. England is through. All peace in Europe can start tomorrow if you sign this document admitting England has lost the war."

Churchill replied, "I can not sign your document. I do not agree with your assessment of the situation. England has not lost the war."

Hitler began to lose his temper. "Outrageous! Are you blind? Look at the facts!"

Churchill quietly sipped his tea and then said, "In England, we often settle a disagreement by having a contest. Would you consider having a contest with me? The loser will agree that he has lost the war."

"What's the contest?" asked Hitler.

Churchill motioned towards the carp pool. He then said, "The first one who can catch a carp without using traditional fishing equipment is the winner."

Hitler accepted the terms and immediately pulled out his gun and began firing at the carp. The water deflected the bullets and Hitler came up empty-handed.

Hitler then looked at Mussolini. "I hear you are a great swimmer. Get in that pool and get me a carp!" Mussolini desperately tried to grab hold of a carp but their slimy skin kept sliding between his fingers. Finally, an exhausted, wet, dejected Mussolini climbed out of the pool.

Hitler glared at Churchill. "If you think you can do better, then go to it." Churchill calmly dipped his teaspoon into the pool and tossed the water over his shoulder. He then repeated the process again and again.

A frustrated Hitler screamed at Churchill, "What do you think you are doing?"

Not even looking at Hitler, Churchill said as he continued to dip water out of the pool, "It may take quite a while but we will win this war."

POWER NUGGET #91:

Being judgmental comes from a lack of trust.

I want you to think about someone you trust. Is that a person you would allow to borrow your car? The answer to that is probably yes. How about a stranger? Would you allow that person to borrow your car? Probably not unless the circumstances were extraordinary. Why is the answer different? Because one has earned your trust and the other has not. It's not that the other person is a bad person, it's just that you do not know him.

What about the person who has wronged you? Does that person deserve your trust? Maybe, maybe not. It depends whether it was a one time situation or whether the situation occurs over and over again. The challenge here is to keep from being judgmental of this person. Many times when we don't trust someone who has wronged us our anger turns into judgment. This is a dangerous path to walk.

So, what is the answer? Forgiveness towards the person and the willingness to take a chance on trust. Forgive the person who has wronged you and give him/her another chance. What about strangers? We need God's wisdom and discernment in trusting them. I think in most cases we will know whether their motives are pure or not. As the Bible says, by welcoming strangers some have entertained angels.

POWER NUGGET #92:

A friend is a special gift from God.

It was the great George Washington who said, "True friendship is a plant of slow growth, and must undergo and withstand the shocks of adversity before it is entitled to the appellation." How right he was. True friendship takes time to build. It takes commitment. It takes trust and belief in each other. A true friend cares and puts the other's needs first.

History tells us the story of two such friends. Their names were Damon and Pythias. They lived in the fourth century B.C. Damon and Pythias started their friendship as children and the bond between them grew and grew throughout the years.

Pythias was becoming known for the great speeches he was giving. He was telling the public that all men had the right to be free. He also said that absolute tyrants should never be kings.

Dionysius, the ruler of Syracuse, heard about the speeches of Pythias. Dionysius became very angry and had Pythias and his friend Damon brought before him. Dionsysius yelled, "Why are you doing this? Who do you think you are, creating unlawful thoughts among my people?"

"I speak only the truth and there is no law forbidding that," said Pythias in a calm voice.

"And do you still believe your 'truth' that a king who has too much power should not rule?"

"If the people did not give the king this power then that is what I believe," said Pythias.

"You have spoken treason! Take back what you have said or be willing to pay the price for such disloyal talk."

"I will take back nothing I said," said Pythias.

"Then you must die," said Dionysius. "Any last requests?"

"Yes," answered Pythias. "Let me go home and say good-bye to my wife and family and also prepare my household affairs."

"So, you think me to be an idiot as well as a tyrant. If I let you leave I will never see you again."

"I promise you I will return," said Pythias.

"You have given me no reason to think you will keep your promise."

At that moment, Damon stepped forward and said, "I will be his reason. You may keep me in jail until he returns. You have heard of our friendship. With me in your custody you can be sure Pythias will return."

Dionysius looked at Damon, "If he doesn't return then you must be willing to die in his place."

Damon answered the ruler with complete confidence, "My friend Pythias will keep his promise."

Pythias was let free to settle his affairs and say good-bye. Damon was thrown in jail. After many days and no sign of Pythias, Dionysius could not resist the temptation to gloat. He went to Damon and said, "Your time is almost up. You were a fool to trust your friend to sacrifice his life for you. You most certainly will die in his place."

"You are wrong," said Damon. "He has simply been delayed. I believe in my friend. I trust my friend. If it is humanly possible then he will come."

The day came for the execution to take place. Still there was no sign of Pythias. Damon was brought to the place of execution. Dionysius looked at Damon with a sly grin and asked, "What do you think of your friend now?"

"I trust my friend," said Damon.

At that very moment, the doors were flung open. Pythias staggered into the room about ready to collapse from exhaustion. He was bruised and battered and could hardly support his own weight as he ran to his friend. Pythias said, "I am glad you are safe. I feared the worst. My ship was wrecked and then I was attacked by robbers. But I didn't give up. I kept the faith. And I have made it in time. I am ready to receive my sentence of death."

Dionysius was touched by this display of loyalty. His heart was softened and he felt the love between these two friends. Dionysius said, "You are pardoned. I never thought it possible to have such trust and love in a friendship. You have shown me I was wrong and I will reward you with freedom. I do, however, have a request from you."

The two friends looked puzzled at the change in Dionysius. "What can we do for you?" they asked the ruler.

With an open heart Dionysius said, "Teach me how to be a part of a friendship such as yours."

WOW! That's what friendship is all about. That story reminds me of my very best friend. He died on a cross around 2,000 years ago so I could live. His name is Jesus Christ and He not only is my very best friend, He is also my Lord and Savior.

POWER NUGGET #93:

Keep smiling, God is always with us.

Did you realize that the muscles that form a smile release a chemical in our bodies that make us feel good? Isn't that wonderful and amazing? God has thought of everything. One of the things He thought about was being able to be everywhere at one time. God is Omnipresent. Since God is everywhere at the same time then we are never alone. That is a very comforting truth for me. God is always watching over us and He knows what are needs are and How to fill them. So, keep smiling, God is always with you.

POWER NUGGET #94:

How can I feel better when I am depressed or frustrated? One way is to think about someone who is hurting more than I ... and figure out a way I can help that person.

Were you ever bored as a child? When you were, what did your mom or dad tell you to do? They probably told you to go do something. When we took their advice we discovered that we weren't bored anymore. The same is true when we are depressed or frustrated. We are focusing too much on ourselves. When we do this, it makes the situation worse. But there is a way we can help ourselves and other people. Think of someone who is hurting and figure out a way to help him overcome his pain. When you do this you accomplish two things. One, you ease the pain of another person. Two, you help ease your own pain. You take the focus off yourself and your challenges don't seem so magnified. When a problem is not magnified it is easier to handle. So, go out there and find some needs and fill them and you will soon discover that your needs are filled too.

POWER NUGGET #95:

The marriage is the glue that binds the family together.

Jan Northington shares a touching story of how Jesus taught her the secret to a successful marriage. It had been a rough night. She and her husband had had a terrible argument. Now, even though it was hours later and the morning after, Jan still felt the sting of their words.

That morning, Jan's husband tried to start things anew. "I'm ready to move on if you are. I do love you." The words meant nothing to Jan. They didn't feel genuine. They were just words do her.

Just then, shouts came from the children's room. "He took my Legos. He didn't even say 'Please.'" Daniel desperately wanted to keep his brother from playing with his new toy.

Jan went to the entrance to the children's room and said, "Daniel, can't you let Philip play with them for a while?"

"I don't want to share. I don't want him playing with them."

Jan sat her little boy on his bed and reminded him of the story they had read last night and the question they had asked, "What would Jesus do?" She explained to Daniel that Jesus wants us to forgive and give even when we don't feel like it. Her words stung her own heart. She was doing the same thing with her husband as Daniel was doing with Philip. Jan and Daniel talked that it is sometimes hard to forgive and share with the "big" things in our lives but that Jesus will help us change our hearts. "What would Jesus do, Daniel?"

Without hesitation Daniel said, "He would forgive Philip and let him play with the Legos. He would probably even play with him." Daniel looked at Philip and said, "Philip, you can use my Legos tomorrow." Daniel then got up and looked at his mother, "I will be back. I need to go ask Jesus to change my heart for today."

Jan was tremendously touched by her little boy. She knelt beside his bed and tearfully prayed to Jesus to change her heart toward her husband ... today. The peace of God came over her as forgiveness and love for her husband and herself came into her heart.

Daniel came back into the room and said, "Philip, you can use my Legos all day if you want to." There was a change in Daniel. Was it the neighbor children who came over to play or was it the touch of God? Jan hoped her little boy had had the same kind of conversation with the Lord as she had just had.

Jan and her husband's eyes met. He said, "It is a good thing I have to go to work today. It looks like you have your hands full with all these children. All you would need is one more 'child' around the house." A connection was made. Understanding, love, and forgiveness flowed between husband and wife. Jan looked at her husband and said, "I do love you and I am ready to move on too."

The marriage is the glue of Jesus Christ that holds the family unit together. If the glue is strong then the family is strong. If the glue is weak then there is pain, heartache, and many times divorce. Let Jesus Christ be the glue to bind your marriage and family together.

POWER NUGGET #96:

The family is the glue that binds society together.

Just as the marriage is the glue for the family, the family is the glue for society. Every society in history which has been strong and prosperous has been so because the family was strong and prosperous. I am not necessarily talking about prosperous in money but prosperous where it counts: character, integrity, love, commitment.

What caused the fall of the Roman Empire? The Roman Empire fell after the family had already fallen. The Roman society began to falter morally. They began to do disgusting, sinful things. These sins probably included adultery, murder, homosexuality, etc. When sin begins to overtake a society it then puts tremendous stress on the family unit. Divorce runs rampant in the society creating a chasm within the family. New laws are put in action which support this severing of the family. Before long, the society is gone. When the family unit is pulled apart then the society will crumble every time.

So, where does America stand? What is her future? Well, if we modeled history, then it doesn't look good. Immorality has began to consume our society. We have couples living together out of wedlock. Adultery has become the pastime of many. We have young boys getting young girls pregnant and then leaving that girl and the child inside her to fend for themselves. Even worse, we have children being murdered for the sake of convenience all in the name of a euphemism — ABORTION! This is just to mention a few of our problems. So, what is America's future? It depends on the people. If America will turn away from her sinful ways and come back to "one nation under God" then she will be saved. It all begins with the individual human heart. Who controls your life? Whom do you serve? Americans must address these fundamental questions. These are the questions of life. For me, I know the answers to these questions. I speak as Joshua in the Bible when he said, "But if you don't want to serve the Lord, you must choose for yourselves today whom you will serve.... As for me and my family, we will serve the Lord" (Joshua 24:15 NCV).

POWER NUGGET #97:

I have a dream! My dream is alive! I will keep on keepin' on! I will not quit until the job is done!

In order for you and me to live our dreams, we must stay focused on the end result. That is why positive affirmations such as the Power Nugget above are so important. Reminding ourselves of this affirmation on a consistent basis will help provide the motivation we need to persevere to the end.

There is a the story of a young man of Italian heritage. This young man had a dream. His dream was to visit his homeland of Italy. So, he saved his pennies and dimes and eventually he had enough money for the trip. The young man planned a great adventure and was ready to leave for his trip.

Before he left, the young man decided he could use a haircut. The young man went into the barbershop and began telling the barber all about his upcoming adventure. Being a negative man, the barber began to spew out his negativism. "How are you going to get over there to that Italy place? It can't be easy!"

"I am going to fly Alitalia airlines," said the young man.

"That's a terrible idea," said the barber. "They have got an awful reputation. Well, if you ever get there, where are you going to stay?"

Very excitedly the young man answered, "I am going to stay at the Hilton in Rome."

"Forget that! It's a terrible idea. They have awful service. Well, what are you going to do when you get there?"

With even more excitement the young man said, "I am going to see the Pope."

"The Pope? That's a terrible idea! You can't see the Pope. He only sees important people." With that the barber looked the young man up and down. "And that doesn't appear to be you!"

Well, despite all this negativism the young man went on his trip and he had a wonderful time. When he got back home it was about six weeks later and it was time for another haircut. The young man walked into the barbershop and the barber immediately began to gloat. "So, I bet you never did get over there to that Italy place."

"I sure did," said the young man. "I had a wonderful time. I flew Alitalia airlines and they were great. We were on time the entire flight and service was awesome. When I got there I stayed at the Hilton and they treated me like a king. They gave me a suite and took care of my every need. I then went and saw the Pope and I kissed his ring."

"You did?" gasped the shocked barber. "Well, what happened? What did he say?"

"Well, the Pope looked down at my head and he said, 'Son, where did you get that terrible haircut?' "

We need to be exactly like this young man. We need to ignore any negativism around us (which sometimes is inside our own heads) and focus on the possibilities. This Power Nugget will help us do just that.

POWER NUGGET #98:

We can not truly help someone until we can move beyond sympathy to empathy.

What is the difference between sympathy and empathy? Well, sympathy deals with feeling and empathy deals with understanding. One of the reasons our government is not helping as many people as it should is because many of our leaders and the mainstream press are full of sympathy and not empathy. I think most of them mean well, it is just they don't have the understanding of how to help.

Let's say we have a family who is in desperate need of our help. We go to their house and we cry with them. That's fine in the very beginning. But after six months we are still crying with them. We are still saying things like, "Oh, I feel so bad for you! The children are starving! You are going to be homeless! I feel your pain!" Now, let me ask you a question. Are we truly helping this family? The answer is no. It is time to move from sympathy (feeling) to empathy (understanding). We need to make tough decisions to help people.

Let's take welfare. Is it helping people? For a few, yes. For many, NO! Is it hurting them? For many, YES! How is it hurting anybody? Because it is making them dependent on the government. Because it is helping people to be lazy (we have people watching soap operas not trying to get a job while you and I through our tax money pay for them to do this — THIS IS WRONG). Because it is not helping people believe in themselves and the God-given abilities that they have. We have to toss the current welfare system out the window and create a brand new system which truly helps through empathy not sympathy.

Some of you might be saying, "Okay, Mark, I agree with you. But I am not in government so what does this mean for me and my family?" Well, let's say your daughter comes home with a big problem. She asks for your help. How are you going to help? Will you just sit and cry with her? Or will you maybe do a little crying, seek to truly understand, and with God's help come up with a solution? The answer is you will probably choose the second approach to help your daughter.

The point I am trying to make is that sympathy and empathy are both good emotions. But to truly help we have to move through sympathy to empathy where solutions are born.

POWER NUGGET #99:

Congruency is the portrait of a champion.

Have you ever wanted to get in shape but at the same time would rather sit on the couch with a bag of potato chips watching your favorite television show? Have you ever wanted to boost your career but find yourself thinking only of weekends and vacations? If your answer to either of these questions was "yes" then you have incongruency in your life. But don't worry, we all probably have some incongruency in our lives. What we have to do is make sure we are congruent where it really counts. We can do this by taking another look at our goals. What are your goals? What do you have to do to accomplish them? Where (if any) do you have incongruencies which are holding you back? The answers to these questions will help you stay on track and sprinting towards the finish line of your goals.

One area that we must always stay congruent is with our values. Incongruency with our values creates inner confusion and conflict. It also frustrates and confuses the people around us. Integrity is congruency in talking and living the values of the Holy Bible. If ever in doubt, then get in the Word. Staying focused and congruent with God gives us focus and success in life.

POWER NUGGET #100:

A champion is honest with him/herself and admits when he/she is scared, but then the champion goes forward and faces that fear.

Fear can be one of the most crippling emotions we can ever experience. Fear can also be one of the most exasperating emotions. The champion has learned to use fear to improve life. For most people, fear is not a pleasant experience, but it can be a prospering one. For example, fear warns us of danger. Fear also can be a motivator to get us to take the actions we need to take. The champion has learned to make peace with his fear.

It was Emerson who said, "If you do the thing you fear then the death of fear is certain." When you truly look at your fear, many times you will discover that its "bark is worse than its bite." You see, most of our fears have no teeth. We need to face our fears. And if we discover that they are toothless, then we can burst through that fear. If you discover your fear does have some teeth, then analyze it. Is it anything to be afraid of? Can it hurt you? How can you burst through this fear victoriously? These questions will help you find the answers you need to conquer fear the way you were meant to — as a champion.

POWER NUGGET #101:

Faith is a power that is unseen but always is heard.

What was it that gave David the strength to defeat Goliath? What was it that gave Dr. Robert Schuller the courage to build the Crystal Cathedral when he didn't know where the money would come from? The answer of course is faith. We are nearing the end of this book. This book has been all about faith. Faith for me to write it. Faith for you to read it. Faith for us both to learn from it.

Think about the goals you wrote down during our goal setting process. Some of them probably seem a little overwhelming. Maybe even impossible. But I am a living example of what is possible through faith in God. At the beginning, writing this book was overwhelming. But now it is almost done. So, keep your eyes on your goals and believe they are completed. As it says in the only book without error (The Bible), "... All things are possible for the one who believes" (Mark 9:23 NCV).

CONCLUSION

Well, there you have it, 101 Power Nuggets. I hope you have enjoyed your journey through this book. More importantly, I hope you have found it helpful, motivational, and inspiring. I am convinced that if you adopt these Power Nuggets into your life you will discover a brand new world of success. Even the most successful person can improve, and isn't that what life is all about? You may be nearing the end of the journey of this book, but your journey of life is ever beginning. Trust in Jesus Christ and He will take you all the way. God bless you always!

SUGGESTED READINGS

I think you will find the works listed very helpful. In fact, many of the stories found in *Power Nuggets*, I learned about through some of these works.

*The *Bible*

In Search of the Blessing by John Trent and Gary Smalley

The Book of Virtues and *The Moral Compass* edited with commentary by William Bennett

The Power of Positive Thinking by Norman Vincent Peale

Over The Top by Zig Ziglar

Chicken Soup For The Soul series of books by Jack Canfield and Mark Victor Hansen

Awaken the Giant Within by Anthony Robbins

Stories For The Heart compiled by Alice Gray

Don't Sweat The Small Stuff ... and it's all small stuff and *Don't Sweat The Small Stuff with Your Family* by Richard Carlson, Ph.D.

A Treasury of Humor edited by Eric W. Johnson (Amherst, NY: Prometheus Books). Copyright 1989.

Podium Humor by James C. Humes

Tough Times Never Last, But Tough People Do! by Robert H. Schuller

No Wonder They Call Him The Savior by Max Lucado

Ordinary Men, Extraordinary Heroes by Dexter Yager and Ron Ball. This book has valuable information for the man wanting to be his best. This book and *The World Book Encyclopedia* are where I got my information on "The Battle of Waterloo."